INTRODUCTION TO CLAY SHOOTING

INTRODUCTION TO
CLAY SHOOTING

JOHN FLETCHER & PHILIP UPTON

ARGUS BOOKS

Argus Books Limited
1 Golden Square
London W1R 3AB
England

ISBN 0 85242 918 5

Phototypesetting by TNR Productions, 19 Westbourne Rd,
London N7 8AN, England
Printed and bound by LR Printing Services Limited, Manor Royal,
Crawley, West Sussex, RH10 2QN, England

CONTENTS

FOREWORD

by A. J. Smith, World FITASC Sporting Champion 1987

Clay shooting has given me tremendous pleasure in the last 10 years, so I was pleased to be given the opportunity to write the foreword for this book, which I hope will introduce many newcomers to the sport.

I have been lucky in that I have enjoyed a fair measure of success in the sport. I have represented England in the Commonwealth Games and Great Britain in World and European Championships for Olympic Trap, and my proudest moment came when I received the European FITASC Sporting Championship gold medal in 1985.

But even without achieving those kinds of success, clay shooting is still a tremendous sport that you can enjoy at any level of ability. I still get as much pleasure from attending local shoots as I ever did, because the atmosphere of friendly rivalry is one that I have never really come across in any other sport.

If you watched the recent *Star Shot* series on BBC2 you will have seen me and some of the other top clay shooters in this country competing in teams with stars from the broader sporting world such as Ian Botham and Bob Champion. I thoroughly enjoyed it and, if watching it has made you think you would like to know more about the sport, you can do no better than to read the *Shooting Magazine Introduction To Clay Shooting.*

It is aimed at beginners, and John Fletcher and Philip Upton have used all their considerable experience in producing *Shooting Magazine* every month, to produce an introduction to the sport that tells you what you need to know – but which does not baffle you with too much science.

I hope you take up the sport – and that one day we will meet in competition!

1 INTRODUCTION

Modern clay pigeon shooting has absolutely nothing to do with pigeons – or even clay if it comes to that. The targets used in this fast growing and exciting sport are circular, ashtray-like domed discs, generally made from chalk and pitch, and there are many in the sport who prefer to talk about clay target shooting or simply clay shooting. The latter is the simpler description and is the one which we will use throughout this book. Apart from anything else, it involves no association at all with the more contentious, and very different, area of live bird shooting.

THE ORIGINS OF CLAY SHOOTING

The sport of clay shooting can be traced back to the latter part of the 19th century, when shooting live pigeons, or sparrows and starlings for that matter, was a popular sport. It was eventually banned in this country in 1921, although it is still popular in some parts of Europe and vasts amounts of money can still be made or lost in betting on the sport.

The idea with live bird shooting was to shoot the birds as soon as possible after they were released from 'traps' in front of the shooter, so that they fell within a perimeter fence. Shooters were handicapped according to ability by being asked to stand further away from the traps.

Apart from its rather grisly atmosphere, this sport had other disadvantages – not the least of which being the time and trouble involved in trapping suitable numbers of live birds – which encouraged enthusiasts to find an alternative inanimate target.

There were numerous experiments with various inanimate targets – for example, glass balls stuffed with feathers – and equally odd machines to propel them into the air. But the

The pavilion at Bisley Gun Club is one of the most attractive in the country.

breakthrough from which all modern clay shooting sprung came in 1880, when an American called George Ligowski saw some youths skimming clam shells off some water. He appreciated the shells' aerodynamic qualities and it was not long before he had the idea of making flying discs out of clay.

These early targets were made entirely out of baked clay and would have been far harder to break than those which we are used to nowadays. It did not take long to come up with the basic formula used today but even now different clays from different manufacturers that have been stored in different conditions may be very much harder to break than others.

The basic requirements, of course, are that a clay should be breakable with three or four pellets from a shot load and that it should be strong enough to withstand the shock of being 'thrown' from the arm of a trap which may be geared up to throw it over 130 metres. Originally all clay targets were black, but nowadays shoot organisers use all kinds of different colours to help the clays stand out against various backgrounds.

In America clay shooting caught on quickly. By 1892, 30 million clay targets were used in just one year, but it was far slower to catch on in Great Britain. Here just about the only people offered the opportunity to shoot clays were the upper classes and they were happier shooting game or, if they were of a competitive disposition, live pigeons.

Even so, Britain did have an association to look after the administration of the sport – the Inanimate Bird Shooting Association – and it held its first championship meeting at

Holland & Holland's Shooting School has introduced many newcomers to the sport.

Wimbledon in July 1893. There were 44 entrants and the traps were set at 18 yards distance. It was won by Mr J. Izzard with a score of 9 out of 10 – which bears little comparison with the 100 out of 100 which is virtually essential these days if a shooter is to win a major shoot in the 'Down-The-Line' discipline which is the closest equivalent to the shooting in those far off days.

By 1904 the organisation had become known as the Clay Bird Shooting Association, but the sport still remained basically the preserve of a few well-off enthusiasts. In 1908 trials were held at Uxendon for teams for the Olympic Games, and the English gun trade were using shooting schools – and clay targets – to allow customers to try their guns and get their hand in for shooting 'the real thing'.

There was a break for the 1914-18 war and in 1925 there was the first ever Sporting Championship. This is the form of clay shooting in which the targets are thrown in a tremendous variety of ways – at different heights, speeds and angles – and which has become by far the most popular form of the sport in Great Britain. Originally the idea was to simulate the flight of live birds – but the ingenuity of modern shoot designers has left nature trailing far behind!

By now automatic traps were in use too, allowing a far more rapid form of competition, and there were 238 clubs in the country by 1929. The sport was administered by the British Trap Shooting Association now, and international matches had already started between the home countries.

A good deal of the driving force behind clay shooting in those early days came from Nobel Industries – part of ICI and pro-

Some clubs have rather rough and ready facilities!

ducers of Eley ammunition. Their commercial interest in the sport was obvious and the company remained heavily involved in the organisation and funding of clay shooting until relatively recently.

Currently the sport is administered largely by the Clay Pigeon Shooting Association (CPSA), with the Scottish, Welsh and Irish having their own independent and much smaller associations. The CPSA is now an independent body funded largely from its membership – around 17,000 people at the end of 1986 – and by Sports Council grants. Originally, though, the CPSA was financed entirely by Nobel Industries – and Eley Ammunition are still major sponsors at many top national championships.

The sport today

Clay shooting today is by no means simple to describe. It is not a unified activity like golf, football or squash, for example, and it actually comprises a tremendous variety of different disciplines, each with different rules and often with different intentions.

There are three 'basic' forms of the sport – Skeet, Trap and Sporting – but these are sub-divided into at least eight distinct 'disciplines', as they are known. We'll deal with those in a later chapter, but it is sufficient to say for now that all of them involve the basic task of trying to break a clay target by shooting at it with a shotgun.

Clay shooting is a sport that people go into with very different ambitions, and therefore very different requirements. Some shooters want nothing more than the opportunity to meet a few friends every week, or maybe every month, to fire off a few cartridges in the hope of hitting a clay or two and then to adjourn to the nearest pub for a couple of drinks.

At that level the sport is only as demanding as you want it to be. It need not be very expensive – and it should be relatively easy to find a club even if you live in a major city or town, provided you do not mind driving a few miles.

At the other extreme clay shooting offers intense competition at Olympic, World and European level. This type of shooting requires tremendous dedication and, at least in the early stages, the outlay of considerable sums of money, but the rewards are never likely to move you into the Tony Jacklin or Ian Botham category. British shooters do enjoy occasional success in the hard world of international Trap and Skeet shooting, however, which is a commendable achievement in the face of far more professional competitors from Italy, France, the USA and the Iron Curtain countries.

In between these extremes lies a great wealth of national and local competitions. To excel in these requires great ability and dedication, too, but the rewards can be considerable.

No doubt as a legacy of its gambling origins most clay shoots charge an entry fee which covers the cost of putting on the event plus a percentage which is paid back to the most successful shooters as prize money. Prizes for the winner – or High Gun as he or she is known – can often exceed £100 for an entry fee of less than £10, so it is possible to show a good profit on an event.

A skilled and determined 'pot-hunter' might be able to win a few hundred pounds in an afternoon by plotting his timetable carefully and shooting to the limit of his ability, but it is worth remembering that to have reached this level he will have spent many years 'paying his dues' around the circuit. The number of clay shooters who even 'break even' over a season can probably be counted on the fingers of one hand and even they will find it hard to string a few such profitable seasons together.

Newcomers to the sport, or those who simply have less ability, are not expected to compete head-to-head with the aces. All major events are broken into four classes, based on

Helpful advice is readily available to all novice clay shooters.

shooters' average scores, with additional categories for juniors, ladies and sometimes veterans.

Even if you win absolutely nothing in a season that includes most of the major championships in your chosen 'discipline' – or disciplines – it need not cost a fortune. Certainly many people will happily spend as much on golf, sailing or fishing, for example, and anyone who has been to a clay shoot will know that it is not particularly a sport for the rich.

How you approach the sport should determine how much you need to spend on it. If you fall into the category described earlier – a purely social shooter – there is little point in spending a fortune on an expensive, specialised gun or absolutely top quality amunition.

If you have Olympic ambitions, however, there is little point in handicapping yourself by shooting a gun that resembles two drainpipes bolted to a plank of wood. This subject is covered in-depth in a later chapter

A sport for all

Perhaps the latest phenomenon to hit clay shooting – and it has happened only in the last year or two – is that it has become 'trendy'. Until very recently indeed clay shooting was basically a sport that was attached to, if not actually part of,

A group of shooters swapping yarns at the end of a shoot. Above all, clay shooting is a sociable sport.

the country scene. Now, like green wellies and waxproof jackets, it has been taken up by a certain class of well-to-do city dweller.

Much of this may well be due to a rapid recent growth in the number of companies using clay shooting as a form of client or staff entertainment. There is now a plethora of agencies which will run a day's clay shooting for groups of 10, 20 or up to 40 people – with a decent lunch, drinks, tuition and guns and amunition thrown in – as an alternative to a day at the races or a session on a golf course.

It is fun, it gives people the chance to do something that many of them have never done before, and it cashes in on the simple fact that if you put a gun in someone's hands you can virtually guarantee that they will want to make it go 'bang'.

It is also a fact, however, that clay shooting is by no means as easy as it looks – and many of those who first try it on a company day discover that they have been bitten by the bug, and they eventually turn up at their local gun club or shooting school.

A sure sign of this new trendiness has been the number of television advertisements recently which use clay shooting as part of their message. Indeed, clay shooting has even appeared as a sport in its own right recently, either as 'celebrity' events involving members of the Royal Family and stars of stage and screen or more particularly in the form of the BBC's *Star Shot* series of programmes. The first two of these were shown at the end of 1986, with a full series following later in 1987.

Star Shot is the brainchild of David Maxwell – a Scottish international shooter and television cameraman. It is a completely new form of shooting designed specifically for the small screen. It makes exciting television and there seems little doubt that it, or varations on it, could take clay shooting into a completely different era.

Already there are signs that this is happening. Clay clubs, for example, have traditionally been scruffy establishments with the emphasis on providing reasonable shooting conditions with little eye to creature comforts. Catering might aspire to a bacon sandwich and a cup of tea, for example, but it might stop far short even of these unrefined standards.

Now there are plans for a number of far more ostentatious clubs which will rival the best golf clubs in the overall standard of their amenities. There is a very sophisticated clay shooting school at Gleneagles Hotel already and it seems certain that there will be many more to follow.

In fact clay shooting is becoming even broader in its scope. It offers a sport for people from all walks of life and of all ages – who can follow it with single minded intensity or casual enjoyment.

But as an ever-growing band of people are finding, there is a rare satisfaction in the precise co-ordination of eye and hand required to break a clay, and even more so in doing it repeatedly. There is also an undoubted sensuous pleasure in handling the smooth surfaces and well balanced weight of a decent shot gun – and a destructive thrill in hearing it go bang and seeing a clay target explode into a hundred fragments.

In the rest of this book we hope to help you make the most of a potentially addictive sport!

2 HOW TO GO CLAY SHOOTING

The recent boom in clay shooting has resulted in an even larger number of new clay shooting clubs being formed. Never before has there been a better range of clubs and shooting grounds to choose from. Most competitive clay shooting takes place at the weekends, with novices being very well catered for.

Shooting grounds and clay shooting schools are usually open throughout the week for practice and tuition, which can be booked by telephoning the shooting school direct. Anyone new to the sport is well advised to have a few lessons with an experienced clay shooting coach before venturing out on his own.

BACK TO SCHOOL

At the clay shooting school you will be taught the basic safety rules of shotgun shooting, and how to mount and shoot your gun correctly. The coach will also be able to give you tips and advice on how to stand when shooting, and he will cover basic shooting technique. The rest is purely down to practice!

The other way to start clay shooting is to attend a shoot with an experienced shooter who is willing to show the ropes. If you've never fired a shotgun before, do not be tempted into entering a competition for your initiation. It can cause bad feeling with other competitors who are waiting for their turn to shoot a particular stand or layout if you are being coached by a friend and delaying the rest. Some shoots have a novice or 'have-a-go' stand especially for novices. Some clubs also have a qualified coach in attendace who will be only too willing to spend some time with you teaching you the basics of clay shooting marksmanship. These stands are very pop-

Top lady shooter Elaine Foden in action. Most clay shoots have classes for lady competitors.

ular and not too difficult for the novice. Ten clays and ten cartridges plus the cost of the coach for ten minutes costs around £4 – money well spent.

The thrill of hitting your very first clay is unforgettable! Once you have got the clay shooting 'bug', you will be hooked – and the only cure is more shooting! After you have had a couple of goes on the novice stand it is worth going around the main competition course or following a squad of Trap or Skeet shooters from a safe distance to note their various styles. You will also be able to see what actually happens when it comes to your turn to shoot competitively for the first time.

Once you feel that you would like to have a go at a full round of Trap, Skeet or Sporting, the next step is to find a club that is holding a shoot on a particular date. Clay shooting clubs can be found in the most unusual places such as farmers' backyards and even gravel pits!

If you join the Clay Pigeon Shooting Association you will receive a list of CPSA affiliated clubs in your area on request, with telephone numbers and locations of their shooting grounds. It is well worth joining the CPSA, and also investing in an Ordnance Survey map, as some of the clubs are rather obscure and difficult to find. *Shooting Magazine* and *Shooting Times* carry full details of clay shooting clubs and their forthcoming fixtures. If you study the fixtures and see a shoot that is local to you, give the club a ring and explain to them that you are new to the sport and would like to attend. Also ask them if they have any facilities for novices.

Competitive shooting

Clay shooting on a competitive level isn't just for the top shots. Most clay clubs run a novice competition alongside the main event with either cash or trophy prizes. There is no set time for you to arrive, but try to get there as soon as possible to avoid queues and delays. Entry times and closing times vary from club to club and according to the time of year, and it is wise to check in the sporting press or by ringing the club concerned if you are unsure about the start and finish times.

Once you have arrived at the club find the area where entries are being taken. The organising club will ask your name and CPSA number for classification purposes if the shoot is a registered shoot, that is one run under the jurisdiction of the CPSA to ascertain members' annual averages and classification status. If you are a new member you will not have received a classification until you have shot several registered shoots. If you say you are a new member and give the organiser your membership number you will be classified at the end of the day by the club themselves.

If you haven't joined the CPSA and the shoot is a registered event, you can still shoot what is called 'birds only'. This means that all you pay for is the cost of the targets and the

The same shooter mounting the gun to different shoulders. Note how his right 'master' eye pulls the gun over to the right even when shooting off the left shoulder. Establishing which is your master eye is the first step in shooting correctly.

services of the trappers and referees. If you shoot a good score which could put you in with a chance of a prize you won't receive it because you haven't contributed towards the prize money! So it pays to join the CPSA!

A great deal of shoots are advertised as 'open' shoots. This means they are open to anyone who wants to attend – you do not have to be a member of the CPSA. These shoots often attract considerable numbers of entries because of the large cash prizes often involved, although shooters are still put into different classes according to their skills so that the prize money can be divided equally and according to ability. Some clubs now run just two classes, novice and open. The novice class is for shooters who have never won a prize at that particular club before and the open class is for the top shots and for competitors who have been rewarded for good performances. Once the club has established which class or category you fall into, all you have to do is pay your entry fee. Entry fees vary from club to club and according to the number

A coach helps a novice swing onto a high target. Note the use of a semi-automatic, with its low recoil qualities.

of targets involved. There are no set prices and if the shoot is offering considerable cash prizes for the winners you may find that the entry fees are higher.

Once you have paid your entry fee you will be given a score card with your name, CPSA number, if any, and your classification. Some competitors like to have a look at the targets at a Sporting event before they start shooting while others don't bother and just want to get started as soon as possible. The choice is up to you but when you first start competitive Sporting clay shooting try to pick a stand that isn't crowded.

In Trap and Skeet shooting you don't have a choice but it is well worth telling the person handling the entries that you are a novice so you are not put in the same squad as some of the top shots, who sometimes, often wrongly, start to moan and groan that you are delaying the squad.

Before you start shooting, make sure you have enough cartridges with you. If you are going to shoot 25 Skeet, don't take just 25 cartridges, as you may have a misfire or a target will be deemed to be a 'no-bird', a target that is thrown incorrectly, which you may fire at. Always take an extra box of cartridges with you in case such things happen. There is nothing worse than running out of cartridges in the middle of shooting a particular stand or in the middle of a round of Trap or Skeet. Also ensure that you have your score card with you and some waterproof clothing in case the weather takes a turn for the worse.

It is well worth carrying a cloth to clean your gun if it is raining before putting it back into the gun sleeve, and a cartridge extractor in case you have the misfortune to have a cartridge wedged into the chamber. If this misfortune happens to you and you manage to remove the cartridge, either keep it completely apart from the rest of your ammunition or give it to the referee concerned for disposal. Never, repeat never put a dud cartridge back into your gun or mix it with the rest of your ammunition.

When you try competitive clay shooting for the first time, try to pick an event that won't be too tiring. The novice is far better trying a 50 bird Sporting clay shoot than one twice the size, and the same applies to Trap and Skeet. Only by practice and building your own confidence will you feel prepared to tackle the larger shoots. The smaller shoots will also save you a few pounds on entry fees!

A club coach checks the efforts of a novice DTL shooter.

Never feel frustrated if you miss all the targets on one stand at a Sporting shoot. If you do, though, it may be better for you to stop shooting and go back to the shooting school for further instruction. If you hit one or two targets out of ten you're doing well. Low scores mean that you can hit the targets; all that's lacking is the concentration and method to repeat your successes. Clay shooting is very much a matter of practice makes perfect. Only time and a willingness to learn and watch others will help you improve your scores.

Once you have completed the course and your card has been filled in and signed by the referees concerned, return it to the entries supervisor, who will record your score on the scoreboard. Some shooters, including some of our top shots, throw their cards away if they feel they have shot a bad score. Always hand your card in as your score will determine what class you will be in if you return to the same club for another shoot later on. By then you may have improved and your low first score may leave you in a class which you could easily win if you have gained in confidence and your marksmanship has improved.

Some shoots have what is called re-entries. This simply means that you can buy another score card and go around the course again. There has been much debate in the sporting press about re-entry shoots, some in favour, some against. If you feel that you would like another go, fair enough. But some novices will find that their score on the first round, although low, will be even lower on the second. This is where frustration sets in. It is all too easy for a novice's gun handling, and safety, to break down when he gets annoyed.

Never be tempted unless you really feel you could do better. It is probably far better to use the extra money on a visit to the shooting school, who may be able to solve your problems in a few minutes. Never rush, and never push yourself too hard. Clay shooting is an enjoyable sport, so why put extra burdens on yourself?

The cost of shooting

How much does it cost to go clay shooting? The answer to this question rests with the individual concerned. If you can afford it, you could go clay shooting every day of the week, some of our top shots actually do! Apart from the initial purchase of the gun, most of the money is spent on cartridges and entry fees.

Assuming you're going to attend a 50 bird Sporting shoot, what are the typical costs involved? Your average entry fee for event itself could range from £5 up to £10, depending on the prize money at stake. You will need at least 75 cartridges which, on average, could cost you between £2.50 - £3 per box of 25. If you have one entry and take the average cost of a box of 25 cartridges into consideration you won't get much change out of £14. Some clubs try to tempt you by offering reduced fees for re-entries, so you may be tempted to spend more than you originally intended. Most events also have some form of pool shoot, a shoot where you can gamble by trying to shoot the highest score of the day for a small fee, and these can really burn a hole in your pocket if you're not too careful!

Competitive clay shooting can be very expensive if you really get the bug. In the summer months, considerable cash sums are at stake at shoots up and down the country and the competition is obviously very fierce. But clay shooting can also be very cheap and still as enjoyable if you shoot at what is termed 'club' level. Club level clay shooting is dealt with in the following chapter in greater detail but the competitive aspect still remains, but on a far lower key. Shooting against another shooter for a few pounds adds to the excitement of the game.

The competitive edge is a good way of improving your con-

You are never too young to start shooting. This is a young DTL competitor.

centration. If you can master the art of concentration and not think too hard about your misses, you will soon find that your standard will start to improve. All our top shooters had to start from the bottom and work up. One of our top internationals used to shoot for Mars bars to try to improve his concentration and beat his rivals. Now he shoots for several hundred pounds each weekend but he still maintains that the best prize he ever won was his first Mars bar!

The clay shooting bug can grip us all at some time or another. We would all like to shoot as often as possible, but finances and work always seem to get in the way! Clay shooting is one of the most rewarding participant sports available today, and it is one that more and more people are taking a great deal of satisfaction from. Clay shooting is a sport for everyone to enjoy and have a go at. There are no age limits and ladies, juniors and older people are very well catered for. Each month, *Shooting Magazine* keeps all clay shooters fully informed with the latest developments in the clay shooting world. Results and fixtures are published each month, each week in *Shooting Times*, and there's a useful Club Directory with all the details of the various clay shooting clubs in the country, which also appears in Appendix 2 of this book.

By joining a local club you will receive the benefit of fellow members' help and advice on gun selection, cartridges and coaching. You will also be able to enter the club's 'members only' competitions which really are the grass roots of clay shooting and often the best fun. Clay shooting is just like any other sport, the more you put into it the more you get out.

3   CLAY SHOOTING FOR FUN

Shooting a few clays with some friends is one of the best introductions to clay target shooting you can have. Some of the best fun can be found at informal club shoots on a Saturday or Sunday morning where the emphasis is on sport and enjoyment, with the day often ending in the local pub for a few pints and some leg-pulling about the one that got away!

Competition shooting is dealt with in greater detail in Chapter 6, but although competition shooting can be very exciting and sometimes financially rewarding, many people are quite happy to blaze away at clays at the numerous small club shoots across the country. Small club shoots tend to be very informal and are a great way of making new friends with fellow enthusiasts, who are more often than not willing to share their experience with you. You may eventually find that you want to progress into the competitive clay world, but many remain more than happy just to 'smoke' a few clays once or twice a month.

Grass roots shooting

Small clay shooting clubs are often referred to as the 'grass roots' of clay target shooting. They are responsible for producing many of our top shots and champions, and play a considerable role in the promotion of clay target shooting as a sport. Most clubs are run by enthusiasts who help keep the overall shooting costs down to a minimum. The work involved in running the club and setting up the shoots is shared by the members who are all expected to help. By sharing the work load and keeping overheads to a minimum, the members are able to enjoy clay shooting at a budget price.

But one of the big attractions of joining a small clay club is that if you make a complete 'fool' of yourself when you first

Many top shooters start their careers in informal clubs – and the standard can be surprisingly high.

start, nobody is likely to give you a ribbing. Everyone has to start somewhere and you will find that club shooters are some of the friendliest clay shooters around. They will understand how you feel if you miss every target and will try to give you advice on where you are going wrong. Some clubs have their own coach who is usually on-hand to teach new members and novices the basics of clay target shooting. The emphasis of small club shoots is on enjoyment –and the only pressures you may feel is to buy a pint or two at the end of the day!

Unlike competitive clay shooting where considerable cash prizes can be won – even shotguns – small club shoots usually offer small prizes such as trophies or shields to the winners. This is done to keep the shooting costs in reach of everyone, and to keep the crowds of competitive shooters away. Most clubs run a multitude of 'members only' competitions each year. Prizes could be for the most improved shooter of the year, the best lady, junior or veteran – the list of prizes is endless and so is their originality! The High Gun for the day may receive a box of cartridges or points towards an annual competition for the club shooter of the year with the highest points average. Small clay clubs rely on membership participation to survive and all new members will be expected to play an active role, not just in the shooting but also in the clearing up!

Joining a small clay club can be quite difficult. Some are very selective when it comes to accepting new members, and you may have to attend several shoots as a guest. You may then have to go onto a waiting list before you are accepted as a full member. This is done so that the club can always rely upon members to support the shoots and help with the organisation and maintenance. Those who do not can expect to have their membership terminated when the renewal is due. If you arrive when all the setting-up work has been done and leave before the end of the shoot, don't expect a warm welcome next time you attend. Some clay clubs have to restrict membership because of the size of the shooting land available. Don't be put off if you are refused membership at first, ask if you can go onto the waiting list until a vacancy occurs.

Small clay clubs can be found anywhere there is a suitable piece of land to shoot on. Your local gun shop will have the details of most clubs in the area and the name and telephone number of the secretary or person to contact. If you live in an area that seems to be devoid of any clubs, do not despair. You could form your own!

Starting your own club

Starting your own clay club can be very rewarding and sometimes very frustrating. If clay shooters had everything their way, there would be a clay shooting ground with all the facilities every mile or so. But one of the biggest problems facing clay shooting today is noise. Trying to find suitable land to shoot on can be an extremely difficult task and even if you do, it only takes one nearby resident to complain and you have lost your shooting, especially if you shoot too much and too often.

Farmers are usually very understanding people and it's worthwhile looking at local farms to see if there is any suitable terrain. Your task of finding a suitable site can be made a great deal easier if it is split with friends who are keen to help you form the club. A note on your local gun shop notice board or a small advertisement in the local press will put you in contact with fellow enthusiasts who, like you, have nowhere to shoot. Collectively, you stand a better chance of finding suit-

On a permanent layout, safety cages are a good idea.

able land and the basis for starting a club of your own.

If you are lucky enough to find a suitable area to shoot and have agreed with the farmer or land owner concerned when you can shoot and the rent to be paid, the next problem is buying the equipment and taking out the correct insurance cover in case of accidents. The CPSA have several excellent publications dealing with setting up and running clay shooting grounds. They can also offer insurance for members and for grounds. Read the publications very carefully and make sure you are not shooting near any roads or across any public right of way.

Once you are satisfied that all the safety conditions have been fully met, then, and only then, can you start to consider organising your first shoot. If you have a few members who are willing to help in the organisation and running of the shoot, your taks will be made a lot easier. Traps, clays, gun racks, safety cages and a host of other equipment will have to be purchased. By charging a small membership fee and sharing the costs of equipment, the financial burden will not be too bad.

Your biggest capital outlay – apart from the ground rent, if any – will be the cost of the traps to throw the clays. Traps vary in price from £25 for a simple manually operated trap up to several thousand for fully automatic traps. Small clubs usually have a few basic traps which can very easily be adjusted by the members, so that targets of different speeds and angles can be thrown. It would be far better to buy a trap that can throw two clays at varying speeds and angles, than one that is not fully adjustable for speed and angle.

Modern clay target traps are very robust and easy to operate. If you cannot afford to run a new trap, your local gun shop may have some secondhand traps or traps for hire until you have enough money in the club funds to purchase one of your own. Prices vary and it is worthwhile studying the market before purchasing. Simple manually operated traps,that can throw two clays simultaneously, can be cocked easily and are fully adjustable for height and speed, are ideal for clubs with limited budgets. Even though you may only be able to afford one trap at first, you can still set it up and let all the members shoot one stand before changing its position for the next one.

Sporting shooting is the easiest discipline to set up to provide a variety of different targets. Trap and Skeet are more expensive disciplines to install and cannot be dismantled at the end of the day. If you want to shoot Trap and Skeet, unless you are extremely wealthy, you will have to travel to the nearest club which has Trap and Skeet facilities. Sporting shooting is ideal for the small clay club and you can make the targets as easy or as hard as you like by varying the speed, the angle and the distance of the trap from the shooter. Whatever form of shooting you go in for, never leave any traps at the ground unattended – because they will soon be stolen.

Every member should take a turn in trapping. Trapping is very simple provided you follow a few simple guidelines. Make sure that the trap is well away from the direction of the shot and that the trapper is well protected and concealed from any possible danger. Clay targets are released when the trapper hears the world 'pull'. The shooter should only call this command when he is ready to shoot – never before. Always remember to give the trapper enough time between shots to reload. You can reload your gun considerably quicker than a trapper so do not be too quick when calling for another target. Basic safety rules prevail. Trappers should

Facilities can be very basic for Sporting shooting – and can be totally transportable between events.

never leave the trap while shooting is in progress. If something happens, the trapper should wave a red flag above his head while seated, to signify that something is wrong. Never stand up and shout – just wave the flag and draw attention to the rest of the members that you need assistance before shooting can start.

Traps can be dangerous if they are neglected or abused. Never leave a trap unattended and loaded. A blow from a trap arm or from a clay accidentally discharged could result in a serious injury. At the end of each day, traps should be checked and lubricated to prevent corrosion and fatigue. Springs should be slackened so that they do not lose their power and the whole trap assembly should be stored in a safe, dry area. Correctly maintained and used, traps will last for years and only the wearing parts such as the bushes, trap-arm rubbers and springs will need to be replaced.

Cartridges can be expensive to buy – especially in small lots. If you have sufficient numbers, one of the best ways to buy cartridges economically is by the thousand. Most gunshops will give you a discount on bulk cartridge sales which can add up to a significant saving over the year. It may be a condition of the ground's use that only cartridges with felt wads are to be used – no plastic pads. Some farmers have found that plastic wads can damager farm machinery and livestock, as they do not rot like fibre wads. If this is the farmer's wish, make sure it is enforced – the penalties for not doing so are obvious.

The remaining equipment such as gun racks, safety cages, score cards and prizes can either be made by the members themselves or improvised. By pooling your combined resources, you will be surprised just what can be accomplished. Clays can be purchased from your local gun shop or direct from the manufacturers if the order is large enough. Clays come in a variety of sizes and colours and need to be stored in a safe dry atmosphere. Boxes of clays which are left out in the rain or used as seats by the trappers will result in broken clays and extra expense for the members. Some clays can be thrown to resemble a bolting rabbit. These clays are thrown on their edge and bounce and role across the ground. To throw rabbit clays you need a special trap and unless your funds are sufficient to afford one of these traps, the novice is best advised to start with a conventional trap.

Running a small clay target club is not an easy job. The structure of any club is very important and, as we said earlier in this chapter, the success of the club rests with its members. To raise funds to cover the cost of the land rental and to purchase the basic equipment needed to start shooting, most clubs charge an annual membership fee. This fee should mean that the overall costs are divided evenly among the members. Once sufficient money has been raised to buy equipment, the membership fee can be reduced or kept the same to generate working capital for prizes, ground improvements and a reserve for a rainy day.

The club constitution is like that of any other club. Officers will have to be appointed – including a safety officer, who will ensure that members act in a safe manner and that all the trappers are correctly briefed. Once a year, an AGM should be held to discuss club matters and finance and to elect or re-elect committee members. At the AGM it is worthwhile looking at the membership record to see how many members have played an active role in the club's activities during the year. Those who have not should either be expelled or 'invited' to show increased interest in the running of the club.

Whatever the size of the club, it is worthwhile affiliating to the CPSA. Apart from offering very favourable ground insurance rates, the CPSA will be able to supply you with all the help and advice you need to start a clay shooting club. The CPSA is divided into regions and you should try to con-

Trapping is an important part of any club's activities. However informal the club, make sure that the trappers have been well trained.

tact your local regional secretary and invite him to the ground as soon as possible. He will be able to look at the ground's potential, offer tips on safety or trap positions and answer any questions you may have concerning running and operating a clay shooting club.

A word of warning

Once you have found a suitable shooting ground and have established a membership that are keen to help with the running and clearing up, don't be tempted into increasing your shooting days too soon. It is very tempting to go clay shooting every weekend – but others may not agree. A considerable number of new and established clay shooting grounds have been closed due to traffic congestion. If you have 50 members who all shoot regularly and they all arrive in their own cars, the police and your neighbours will not take kindly to having their access blocked with dangerously parked cars. If you have limited parking space ask the members to share a car. It would be a great pity to close your shooting ground through a lack of common sense.

Noise presents a bigger problem. If you shoot once or twice a month, most of the nearby population will tolerate the sound of gunfire on an occasional basis. But if you start shooting at the crack of dawn and continue all day until dusk every weekend of the year, do not be surprised if the residents complain and close you down.

It is far better to shoot little but often. If some of the neighbours complain, listen to their complaints and do not be rude or abrupt. Polite conversation and an understanding of their feelings will work wonders. Again, the CPSA are always on-hand to advise clubs on the best way of setting up the ground to keep noise pollution as low as possible. Should you be in the unfortunate position of having a closure order issued, clubs affiliated to the CPSA can apply to them for help and legal advice to defend the right to shoot. But the simplest rule is do not overdo it.

There will always be times when members want to bring guests. Some clubs have to limit the number of shooters either at the request of the land owner or purely because of the size of the ground. If you allow non-members to shoot, they should be restricted to a specific number dictated by the members of the committee. Some clubs use the one member, one guest per month scheme, which is fair and seems to work well. Visitors should always be accompanied by the member concerned, who is responsible for his or her conduct on the day. The club rules should be fully explained and in some cases the guest may have to satisfy the safety officer that he or she is safe with a gun.

A visitors' book should always be kept up-to-date and visitors should be charged an additional fee for the privilege of shooting. By keeping a visitors' book, potential new members can easily be traced and if the police decide to pay a visit, an up-to-date guest book is one of the best forms of proof that you are acting in a safe and considerate manner.

At the end of each shooting day, do not forget to collect all the spent cartridges, and burn or take home any rubbish. Traps, empty boxes and safety cages should be removed and the whole site should be left as you found it. If you do not, penalties are obvious.

At the end of the year, thank the land owner for letting you use the ground, and a bottle or two around Christmas time never goes amiss. Some farmers are reluctant to accept cash as payment for the rental of the land. If this is the case, offer your services at harvest time or ask if you and the rest of the members can help with any jobs around the farm. Above all, show you are willing, and obey any special instructions imposed.

Finally, a note for the shooting 'widows'. The highlight of many small clubs' year is the annual dinner. Apart from being an ideal occasion to present the various club awards, it is also a golden opportunity to give the shooting 'widows' a good night out – and it also goes a long way to ensure that your shooting will continue on the same basis!

4 BUYING A SHOT GUN

Buying a shotgun is like buying a car – you can choose from a wide variety of models with prices to suit most pockets. But before you can consider buying any shotgun, you must first obtain a valid shotgun certificate from your local police authority. Shotgun certificate application forms can be obtained from your local police station, or your local gun shop may have a few to spare.

The 1968 Firearms Act and the 1982 Firearms Act have made a shotgun certificate a legal requirement for anyone contemplating buying, possessing or selling a new or secondhand weapon. A shotgun is described in the act as a 'smooth bored weapon with a barrel length not less than 24 inches'.

Once you have obtained an application form, take great care to study the notes when completing it. It is an offence to falsify any information and if you are in any doubt about a particular question always consult your local police station. When completing the form, you will require the signature of someone who is not a relation who has known you for the last two years. The ideal people are those in public serice such as doctors, lawyers, bank managers – or your local vicar!

How to apply.
Once you have completed the application form, you should return it to your local police station with the appropriate fee. If your application is satisfactory, you should receive your certificate from the chief police office of the area concerned. Some forces may send an officer around to ask a few questions to clear up any routine matters that they are not quite sure about. Try to be as helpful as possible and answer all the questions they have the authority to ask you.

A shotgun certificate is your right and may not be withheld from you unless you have been convicted of a crime such that the police feel it would threaten public safety if you were issued with one. If your application is refused, you have, by law, up to 21 days to appeal to the Crown Court. If you are a member of the CPSA, you can ask them to appeal on your behalf.

Once your shotgun certificate has been issued, you can buy or own as many shotguns as you like. Every time you buy or sell a shotgun from a shop or private dealer you must produce your certificate. If you are selling, it is your duty to inspect the buyer's certificate for validity. Shotgun certificates are valid for three years and the local police force will send you a reminder about the expiry date. But don't wait for the reminder to arrive if the expiry date is drawing close. It is your duty to renew it, and failure to do so could result in a visit from your local police force to confiscate all your shotguns pending possible legal action.

If you work abroad or away from home a great deal, it is advisable to leave your shotguns with a friend who has a certificate or, better still, a gun dealer for safe keeping – especially if you're waiting for your renewal to come through. When taking your gun out for any sporting purpose, always remember to carry a copy of your shotgun certificate with you. It is far better to carry a copy than the original in case the original gets lost. Along with your shotgun certificate you should also carry a note with your gun's serial number. If you have the misfortune to have your gun stolen, the serial number will be the first piece of information the police will require.

Once you have received your shotgun certificate, you can consider buying your first gun. Shotguns can be divided into three categories – over-and-unders, side-by-sides and semi-automatics. Other types are available such as single-barrelled shotguns, although they have a limited use for clay shooting. So let's take a look at these three different types and their use for clay shooting, and take a close look at the importance of gun fit.

WHAT GUN?

Over-and-under shotguns
The over-and-under shotgun is by far the most popular gun used in clay shooting. As you would expect, over-and-under

shotguns have the barrels on top of one another. When clay shooting first started, the side-by-side shotgun was the most popular gun for the simple reason that it was – and probably still is – the most popular gun for game shooting. Game shooting guns are built to be carried all day – hence their relative lightness. But this light weight is not ideally suited to clay shooting, where you may fire a large number of high velocity cartridges in a day – and a light gun will leave your shoulder rather sore.

The over-and-under shotgun is generally accepted as being the ultimate gun for all forms of clay target shooting. The last 20 years have seen a tremendous change in over-and-under shotgun design to produce guns that satisfy the most ardent shooting tastes. In the right hands, a typical modern over-and-under shotgun is capable of shooting most targets. One of the main reasons is that competition over-and-under shotguns have been designed for a specific purpose and nothing else. Although over-and-unders are also finding favour with game shooters, this is only a spin-off from their popularity as a clay shooting gun.

The modern over-and-under shotgun features a single trigger, unlike a side-by-side which, because of its design limitations, usually has two. The advantage of a single trigger is that you don't have to move your finger onto the second trigger to discharge the second barrel. Good quality over-and-under shotguns also have a barrel selector which allows you to

A complete range of shotguns. Top to bottom: a semi automatic, a pump action, an over-and-under and a side-by-side.

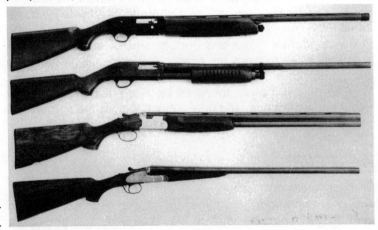

choose which barrel to shoot first. We'll come to the importance of that when we discuss chokes in the next chapter.

As over-and-unders tend to be heavier than side-by-sides, much of the recoil from the cartridge discharge is absorbed, making the over-and-under an ideal choice for the novice or beginner. Most over-and-under shotguns have raised and ventilated ribs which are often available in a choice of different widths to suit the individual. But the deciding factor is that over-and-under shotguns are tailor-made for each of the various clay shooting disciplines. You can choose from Trap guns, Skeet guns and Sporting guns – each designed for a purpose.

Side-by-side shotguns

Side-by-side shotguns are still used by some shooters who want to combine game shooting with clay shooting. If you can only afford one gun, and want to mix both sports, the choice is up to you because the once despised over-and-under is now accepted at even the best game shoots. The side-by-side shotgun has a very limited potential as a serious clay shooting gun. Because of its light weight, the side-by-side shotgun is not really suited to firing the high velocity loads frequently used for clay target shooting today. There is also the tendency for the novice to 'jump' the gun due to its low weight. Jumping the gun simply means that the shooter tries to force the gun in a particular direction rather than letting

The AYA No.2 is an elegant Spanish sidelock side-by-side.

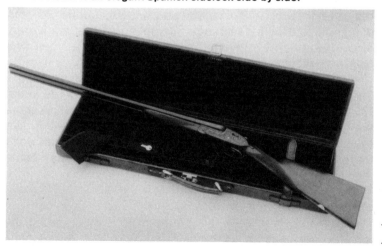

the gun's weight do the work for him. This is where over-and-unders score. Being heavier, the gun's momentum is greater and the swing is a lot smoother than with the side-by-side.

The sighting plane of a typical side-by-side – when you look down the barrels – is very different from an over-and-under. The side-by-side has a very broad sighting plane which tends to make it difficult to track targets accurately. The over-and-under, however, has a narrow single sighting plane which makes it much easier to follow the flight path of the targets.

Semi-automatic shotguns

Semi-automatic shotguns are becoming increasingly popular as a compromise that gives a lightweight gun with negligible recoil. But the big drawback is the fact that you only have one barrel, with no choice of choke. The semi-automatic shot relies on the gas pressure of the first spent cartridge to load the second. All this takes place in a split second while the first cartridge is ejected automatically from the left or right hand side of the gun.

The guns are popular in Skeet and Sporting shooting but have their limitations in all Trap disciplines, where the spent cartridge often lands in front of – or sometimes on – the person about to shoot next to you on the layout. Semi-automatic shotguns are cheap when compared to the conventional over-and-under. This is due to the simple fact that semi-automatics are relatively easy to manufacture and can be completely machine built. Quality and reliability have always been the semi-automatic shotgun's biggest downfall, but modern production techniques and research into auto design have bred a new range of semi-autos that are worthy of consideration by anyone on a low budget or anyone who suffers particularly badly from recoil.

In the right hands, semi-automatic shotguns can be deadly. They are responsible for breaking more Skeet records in the USA than any other gun, and some of our top Sporting shots are finding the semi-automatic shotgun ideal. You either like them or hate them, but when choosing your first gun don't forget the semi-automatic – it's a compromise that could ideally suit you.

Buying a shotgun

When it comes to buying a shotgun for clay shooting the simplest advice is to buy the best you can afford. A well maintained gun is almost indestructible, and although they are prone to rust if not cleaned and oiled after use, they will last a lifetime.

Before you rush out and buy your first gun it is worth doing some homework to establish what type of clay shooting you enjoy. Apart from offering a wide array of different guns, most good gunshops have facilities of their own or with a local clay club or shooting ground where you can try out various guns under expert guidance. Guns today are designed for the 'average' man, but just like clothing, individual sizes do vary and a gun may have to be altered until the fit is comfortable.

Most clay shooters have their guns fitted and the novice will find that a gun that is fitted to his or her own requirements will not only feel more comfortable but will also help to improve his or her marksmanship.

A visit to a shooting school or clay club to be fitted for a gun is just like visiting a tailor. The instructor will arrange for you to have a few practice shots and will teach you the rudiments of gun handling and safety. Once you have fired a few 'dry' shots – without discharging the gun – the instructor will be able to see any areas in gun fit that he feels could be improved.

A coach introduces a novice to a 'try gun' for the first time.

The gun stock could be too long or too short, making it difficult to mount correctly. By standing in front of you with an empty gun raised and pointing at his stretched finger, the instructor will be able to test you for your master eye – the eye you use to see the targets. If the right eye is looking straight down the gun barrel rib with the muzzles pointing directly at the instructor's out-stretched finger, all is well. With a right master eye and shooting from the right shoulder, you should be able to shoot with both eyes open. If you have a left master eye you may find it easier to shoot off the left shoulder. If not, you can try shooting from the right shoulder with the left eye closed.

Once the instructor has coached you he may decide that several alterations will have to be made to your new gun if you are to mount it and shoot it correctly. Most shooting grounds or schools have what is termed a try gun. A try gun is, quite simply, a gun that can be fully adjusted for each individual. The gun stock can be altered for height, length, bend and in some cases width. By watching you mount the gun and fire, the instructor will be able to adjust the try gun to your correct measurements and so improve gun fit and mounting.

If your neck is too long or too short the height of the stock will have to be altered to bring your eyes level with the rib of the gun, for example.

A stock which is too long may have to be shortened by taking away the correct amount of wood from the butt end. If the stock is too short, a piece of wood or a rubber pad may have to be fitted. These pads also serve to reduce recoil, which can be quite painful if you do not hold the gun correctly or if you shoot a large number of cartridges very quickly. In clay shooting you may fire 25 or more shots in just a few minues, which can feel like quite a test if you're wearing thin clothing and your gun is not fitted with a recoil pad.

Apart from checking the height of the comb and the length of the stock the coach will also check to see if you need extra 'cast' on the stock. Modern production guns come with a small amount of cast-off, but some individuals may require more and some less. A gun that has a stock with cast-off allows the shooter to keep his head straight while he places his eye and looks down the centre of the rib. A gun with cast-off means that the gun does not have to be canted and ensures that the eye, the rib and the target are all in line.

Showing where the butt should fit into the shoulder pocket.

Some shotguns have very little or no cast, which makes them difficult for some shooters to aim properly. If the gun is canted to the left to produce a cast-off effect, there is a danger that the shot will go to the left of the target.

Once the shooting instructor is satisfied with your gun mounting and fit, he will record the correct measurements for you to take into your local gunshop, who should be able to make the necessary adjustments. Most gun shops offer a professional gunsmith service and they will give you a rough idea of the costs involved. This is important when taking the purchase price of the gun into consideration. The importance of good gun fit can never be underestimated, and it is far better to have a well fitted budget priced shotgun than an expensive one which is too long, too short, or fitted with a stock that has already been altered for somebody else.

How to choose a gun
Once you have decided to go ahead and buy your first shotgun, contact your local gun dealer who will be only too pleased to discuss your requirements. It is best to visit your gun shop during the week, when the staff will have more time than at the weekend to answer any questions and show you a wide selection of different weapons. One of the first ques-

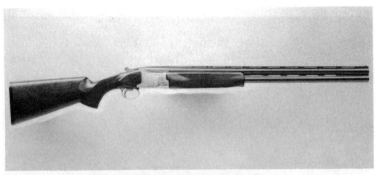

The Winchester 6500 is a popular Sporting shotgun.

tions the dealer will ask is how much are you prepared to spend. He will also ask what type of clay shooting you intend to do. It is pointless buying a Trap gun if you intend to shoot Skeet, although some guns are now available with different sets of barrels and/or a choice of screw-in chokings. If you are unsure about which clay shooting discipline you are interested in, the gun shop will have a range of intermediate guns, commonly known as Sporting guns, which can be used with considerable success for all clay shooting disciplines.

Try to handle as many different guns as possible. Some may look the same but their weight and balance may be completely different. If you show the measurements given to you by the shooting instructor, the staff may be able to narrow the choice considerably. Shotgun prices range from a few hundred pounds to several thousands. Much of the difference in price is due to the cosmetics, such as ornate engraving and fancy woodwork. Although they look attractive, they do not help you shoot any better.

Let us assume that you have £700 to spend on a shotgun. What do you look for, and what shotguns are the best value for money? The first thing to do is work out how much money you have left once the correct alterations, if any, have been carried out by the gunsmith. Ask the gun shop if you can see a selection of guns in your particular price range and handle all of them. Ask the staff what the differences are between each of the various models. One of the most important areas to consider is mechanical reliability. It is pointless buying a cheap gun which may look cosmetically attractive if it keeps malfunctioning and spare parts are hard to obtain.

Most reputable gun dealers will have a good selection of secondhand shotguns on display. Excellent bargains can be had, and do not be put off by any minor dents or scratches in the woodwork. These can usually be rectified if you want, but it is not really worth the additional expense unless it is a very expensive gun. Most secondhand guns will have gone through the gunshop's own workshop before they are put on the racks for sale. If you buy a secondhand gun, the dealer may offer you a limited warranty with the purchase to cover general wear and tear. Ask his advice and follow it. Never be tempted to sacrifice quality for saving a few extra pounds.

The working parts of a modern shotgun are relatively simple, and most of them are contained, hidden from view, in the action. Once you have handled a particular gun that you feel handles well and has a good balance, the next stage is to examine the barrels for any signs of pitting or dents. It is an offence for any gun to be sold – privately or through a gun shop – that does not have up-to-date proof markings. Proof markings mean that the gun has been pressure tested by one of the two Proof Houses in Great Britain. Guns which have passed the Proof House tests are stamped with the appropriate markings of the house concerned on either the barrels or the action. Never buy a gun that is out of proof. If you do and you use it, you are a fool to yourself and a danger to anyone 300 yards around you.

The barrels should be clean and free from any dents or bulges. Small dents or bulges can usually be removed by a gunsmith, but the price of such work should be taken into consideration when negotiating the purchase. When buying a secondhand shot gun, check that the rib is firmly in place and not rusted. Although it is a simple matter to braze a loose rib back in position, the rust can go a lot deeper and could affect the strength of the barrel walls.

Most modern clay shooting guns have single triggers which can usually be adjusted for the weight of pull – the weight needed to pul the trigger to release the firing pin. Ask the gun dealer for some snap caps – dummy cartridges with a spring loaded centre – to check that the firing pins work and the trigger pull. Snap caps will also tell you if the ejectors – the two arms at the breech of the barrels used to expel spent cartridges – are working. Dry firing a new or used shotgun will also tell you if the safety catch is functioning correctly.

Clay shooting guns are fitted with either manual or automatic safety catches. Manual safety catches, which sometimes incorporate a barrel selector, do not re-set to the

The Browning Citori is another popular mid-range gun.

safe area once one or both barrels have been discharged. In competition shooting, it is easy to forget to push an automatic safety catch forward and you may be deducted a target if nothing happens when you pull the trigger because you have left the catch on. Automatic safety catches speak for themselves. Once a shot has been fired and the gun broken, the safety automatically returns to 'safe', and before the next shot can be fired, the safety catch needs to be manually pushed forward. New or secondhand, make sure that the safety catch works. If it does not, have it rectified by the gun dealer.

Once you have checked that the gun functions correctly and are happy with the weight, balance and overall appearance, ask the gun dealer if it is possible for you to try the gun out. He will usually oblige and arrange for you to have a few shots to make sure that everything is functioning correctly. It is a good chance for you to see how the gun performs in the field. If you are happy with the gun, and satisfied with its condition if you are buying secondhand, the next stage is to arrange with the gun shop to have any modifications carried out.

Once the work has been completed, you will have a gun that fits you like a new suit and should last you a lifetime. Never try to cut corners with shotguns. They are lethal weapons in the wrong hands and need to be treated with great care and respect. If your gun has a malfunction, stop shooting immediately. Remove any live cartridges and take it to your gun shop at the earliest opportunity.

Do not wait until Friday to take your gun in for repair if you want to shoot the same weekend. If your gun is in need of repair and you want to use it the following weekend, phone your gun shop and tell them about the problem. It could be something simple that may be solved in a couple of minutes, or it could mean a complete strip down which could involve considerable time in the workshop. If you know in plenty of

Checking the barrel alignment to see which is the master eye. The coach will, of course, have made sure that the gun is empty.

time, you can arrange for a replacement gun or the gun shop – providing they are given plenty of warning – may be able to let you borrow one while yours is being repaired.

The final choice when buying a shotgun rests with you. Always go to a reputable dealer who has a large selection of guns to choose from. Ask as many questions as you like and take any advice offered seriously. Never be tempted by a bargain from a private vendor unless you know the full history of the gun or are accompanied by someone who is conversant with guns. Never buy a gun that is out of proof or a gun that shows visible signs of excessive wear or abuse. Treated with respect and properly maintained, a shotgun will last you a lifetime.

5 CLAY SHOOTING CARTRIDGES AND SHOOTING ACCESSORIES

Buying a new shotgun can be a bewildering task due to the sheer numbers of different models. Just as bewildering is the array of shooting accessories, many of which are essential to good shooting. Spending a considerable sum on a shotgun and then trying to economise on accessories is pointless. The correct shooting accessories can make a considerable difference and it is well worth taking your time in kitting yourself out from head to toe!

CARTRIDGES AND CHOKES

By far the most important shooting accessories – apart from the gun – are shotgun cartridges. The quality of shotgun cartridges is one of the most important factors for successful shooting. Clay shooting revolves around where you place your shot pattern in relation to the target. Poor quality cartridges will produce poor patterns and more missed targets. Good quality cartridges are reliable and will consistently break targets if the pattern is placed in the right direction.

Before we look at shotgun cartridges in greater detail, it is worthwhile taking a look at shotgun chokes, as they play a very important role in the final selection of cartridge and shot size. The type of shot pattern a gun throws is very important. Shotgun patterns are largely determined by the choke at the end of the barrels. The more open the choke, the wider the pattern and vice versa.

For the Trap disciplines, most shooters have fairly tight chokes in both barrels. As the targets are going away from the gun, the shooter needs a tight shot pattern that will only start to get wider when the pattern has caught the target up. The first barrel of most Trap guns is choked fairly tightly, while the second barrel is choked even tighter. This is for the

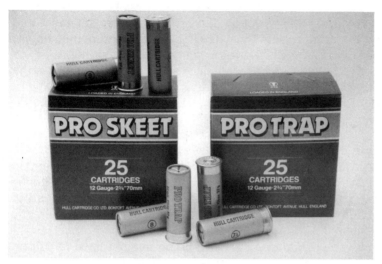

A popular brand of cartridges for Trap and Skeet.

simple reason that if you miss with your first barrel, the pattern needs to be even tighter to catch the target and break it with an effective pattern. Guns with open chokes cannot throw an effective killing pattern at long ranges.

Although most Trap guns have tight choke constrictions, Sporting and Skeet guns tend to be far more open. In Skeet and Sporting, the majority of targets are fairly close when compared to Trap shooting and require the use of more open choke constrictions for effective results. Open bored guns for close targets produce a wide pattern considerably quicker than a gun with tight choke constrictions.

In Trap and Skeet shooting, the choice of chokes is fairly straightforward. Skeet guns need to be as open as possible and, appropriately enough, their choke constrictions for both barrels are known as Skeet/Skeet. Trap guns, as we have already explained, need to be tight because the targets are going away – but what about guns for Sporting?

In Sporting you may have a mixture of targets that are thrown towards you, away from you or across you. The choice of chokes can be bewildering, with some shooters preferring tight chokes and others more open. Modern gun design has resulted in an array of guns that have removable chokes ranging from very open to very tight constrictions. If the targets thrown on one stand are going away you can simply change the choke to suit.

Another help in choosing the right choke constriction is that a large number of shotguns have a barrel selector fitted on the safety catch. By a simple flick of a button, the shooter can choose which barrel is fired first and therefore which choke. If your gun has fixed chokes, you can select either the tighter choked barrel to fire first if a target is going away or thrown at some considerable distance, or the open bored barrel if the target is fairly close.

The debate over which choke is the best will continue to rage. Your local gunsmith will be able to give you information and advice as to the type of choke you need – depending on what type of clay target shooting you intend to do. Chokes can be opened for a small charge by most gun shops but remember that you cannot put back what you have already taken out!

If you stick to one cartridge brand and get used to its performance you will find that your confidence and your ability will grow. If you keep changing cartridges and altering your chokings you may find that your performance and your morale will suffer.

Shotgun cartridges can be divided into three types – Skeet cartridges, Trap cartridges and special high velocity cartridges for FITASC Sporting. Most clay target cartridges have a plastic case, although some manufacturers still produce paper cased cartridges for shooters whose grounds forbid the use of plastic cartridges. The maximum shot size allowed for clay target shooting is English No. 6. The lead pellets must be spherical and made from hardened lead, and may be nickel plated.

The majority of cartridges today use plastic wads, although fibre wads are available. The purpose of the wad is to transmit the power from the charge to the shot and often also to hold the shot in place when it travels up the barrel. The wad size is determined by the cartridge length. The wad has to confine the propellant gases in the chamber until the ignition has built up the correct pressure. There are many different designs of wad, but their various merits are a subject only for the technically minded.

For clay target shooting you can choose between shot size No. 6 to No. 9. The smaller No. 9 shot is commonly used in Skeet cartridges where the shooter wants the maximum shot pattern and spread at relatively close distances. Skeet cartridges when fired from an open bored gun produce an open

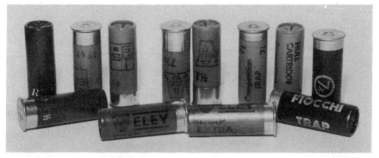

A selection of top clay shooting cartridges.

effective killing pattern at close distances, but soon lose their effective pattern at longer ranges.

Apart from Skeet shooting, Skeet cartridges are commonly used in Sporting for targets that are driven towards you, or for close 'crossers'.

Trap cartridges are also the general all-round cartridges for clay target shooting. Their size ranges from No. 7 up to No. 8, depending on the manufacturer. Most Trap shooting disciplines need a fast cartridge that holds its pattern well.

When you first start clay shooting it is worthwhile buying a few boxes of different cartridge brands and trying them out on a pattern plate to test their performance. In some guns one cartridge may give better patterns than others. Some cartridges – especially the high velocity ones – may cause excessive recoil and make shooting uncomfortable. Only through experiment, using the pattern plate, will you be able to find a cartridge that is low on recoil and produces the best patterns when fired from your gun. Once you have found the ideal gun and cartridge combination, stick to it. The instructor at your local shooting school may be able to help you with pattern testing.

Most cartridges are sold in boxes of 25, although discount will usually be given for orders over 500 or 1,000. To keep the cost of cartridges down, it is worthwhile finding another shooter who uses the same brand and splitting the cost of buying in bulk. Some gun shops only stock certain cartridge brands so it is worth asking your local dealer to keep a supply for you or ask if he can order some for you. Shotgun cartridges should, of course, be kept in a safe dry place and should never, repeat never, be mixed with cartridges of a smaller or larger gauge.

Although modern production techniques ensure that car-

A selection of shooting acessories from Browning Sports.

tridges are totally reliable, there will always be the odd one that creeps through that could be potentially dangerous. Always check each cartridge before loading your gun. If the case is distorted or the cap is malformed, put it to one side and safely dispose of it. Never try to force a cartridge into the breech of your gun, and if you have two guns of a different calibre, store the different size of cartridge separately, to avoid dangerous confusion.

If you are not sure about which cartridge to use, ask the opinion of fellow shooters, who may be able to give you some help and save you considerable expense. A quick look at the spent cartridge cases at the shooting ground will give you a fair idea of which are the most popular clay shooting cartridges around.

Other accessories

Apart from cartridges a good shooting jacket is a must. Just like a suit, a shooting jacket must fit correctly so that it does not impede your gun mounting or swing. Shooting jackets are available in a variety of different sizes and styles. You should be able to find one that fits you correctly, although some jacket manufacturers can also make one to your own requirements.

Five Sporting shooters with different ideas of what jacket to wear for their sport.

Most shooting jackets have two large cartridge pockets on the front which should be capable of holding at least 30 cartridges. An inside pocket is also handy for storing odds and ends such as ear protectors and score cards. The shoulders of the shooting jacket should have some form of pad which should extend right the way down to the pocket so that the gun will not snag when mounting. The most popular pad is made from soft leather with close stitching to prevent the gun catching the end of the material.

When you try on a shooting jacket, do not forget to allow enough room for a jumper or waterproof clothing before making your final choice. Always check that there is plenty of freedom in the shoulders and that the jacket does not impede your swing. A good quality shooting jacket could cost you around £60. This may seem a lot of money, but the quality and the comfort of the fit will repay you many times over.

Waterproof clothing is a must. Apart from the traditional waxproof coats and green wellies, the clay shooter is faced with either getting wet or having to cope with additional layers of bulky clothing. In recent years, lightweight waterproof clothing has been introduced for clay shooters which protects you from the elements and allows complete freedom when mounting and swinging a shotgun. The advantage of

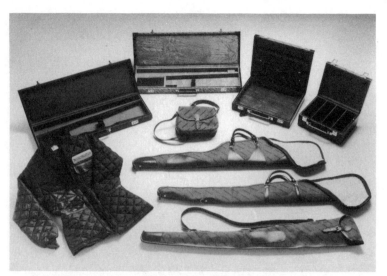

A selection of shooting accessories from Winchester UK.

these lightweight suits is that they can be packed in the bottom of a shooting bag and are ready for use in a few minutes. Suits can range from around £20 up to well over £100 for the specialist garments. But they are worth every penny, especially in competition shooting when the last thing you need is wet clothing and the inherent problems it causes.

Shooting glasses are very important. They have three major functions – all of which can make the difference between a hit or miss. Apart from protecting your eyes from the sun's rays and from pieces of broken or falling clay, good quality shooting glasses can also help to define the target thrown – and the colour.

Broken pieces of clay can be a big problem especially in Skeet and Sporting where the targets are thrown in close proximity to the shooter. Shooting glasses are not sun glasses and may cost considerably more. Some shooting glasses come complete with a selection of interchangeable lenses, which are tinted with different colours to allow the user to select the right lenses for the prevailing conditions.

If you already wear spectacles, a range of special prescription shooting glasses are available with a choice of frames. Never underestimate the importance of good shooting glasses. Apart from helping you shoot better scores in bright light, they could also save your eyesight.

Footwear is very much up to the individual. Any shoe will

do, provided they offer reasonable support and the sole affords good grip in wet weather conditions. When the shooting ground is reduced to a mud bath, you have no choice but to revert to wearing boots of some description. Unless the mud or water is exceptionally bad, ankle boots with a good grip are the best. In fine weather good quality trainers are ideal. Some Trap and Skeet shooters have a special muzzle rest on the top of their shoes. This is to protect the muzzles from any ingress of dirt or obstruction and also helps to keep your trainers or shoes clean from any powder residue.

Carrying cartridges has always proved a problem. Some shooters use a conventional cartridge belt or cartridge bag, while others are more happy to cram as many cartridges as possible into their pockets. The choice is up to you, but a good lightweight holdall which will take cartridges, additional clothing and any other equipment is ideal. In a Sporting shoot you may have to carry up to 125 cartridges, which can be very heavy.

Ear muffs and blinkers help top Trap shooter Chris · Cloke concentrate on the job in hand.

Jonathan Smith uses a Skeet vest, ear muffs and a hat. At Sporting shoots a hat can protect your head from wayward pieces of clay.

Your gun deserves the best protection possible. In the car a rigid gun case with a good security lock is ideal. These cases are usually made from rigid plastic or wood and afford the very best protection when travelling. At the shooting ground, once the gun is assembled you can use a gun slip between stands or squads. Gun slips are cheap and keep your gun clean and dry in between shooting. Most have a carrying sling or handles and the better ones have a fleece lining to help absorb any moisture. All gun slips should have a full length zip so that they can be opened and left to dry after a day's shooting.

A good cleaning kit is a must. You should always carry a basic cleaning kit with you, which should consist of a cleaning rod, oils, a pull-through, a cartridge extractor and some cleaning cloths. Every time you finish shooting, your gun should be given a rub over with an oily rag to remove any moisture and dirt before it is placed in its sleeve or case. Various aerosols are available which make life a lot easier – but never over-lubricate your gun as it could result in a mechanical malfunction or distortion of the woodwork.

One of the most important shooting accessories is hearing protection. It is an unfortunate fact that many clay shooters have impaired hearing due to not wearing suitable protection. Hearing protection is widely available. The most popular kind are the small ear plugs which are light and easy to use, with very little discomfort to the wearer. Some people prefer ear muffs which offer better protection when shooting. Ear muffs should be designed so that they do not impede gun mounting and are comfortable to wear. You can now buy sophisticated electronic ear muffs which allow you to hold a normal conversation with the muffs on, and with a flick of the switch the muffs can be converted into superb hearing protectors while shooting.

Shooting gloves are always worthwhile and should never be omitted from your kit bag. The best are made from thin leather with a silk or cotton lining. Most shooting gloves have a fold-back trigger finger for absolute trigger control and comfort. Make sure that the gloves are well ventilated and have a warm knitted cuff to stop rain and wind. Prices vary but you can expect to pay around £15 for a really good pair.

Headwear may seem superfluous on anything but wet and windy days – and most shooters don't bother at all. But wandering around with a bare head can lead to cuts and grazes from pieces of falling clay – especially at Sporting shoots. The choice of headwear rests with the individual. Some people prefer a hat with a long peak, while some have internal padding to protect the crown. Try as many different shooting hats as possible and once you have found one that is comfortable and fits you well, stick to it.

When you go clay shooting, always go prepared. A set of gunsmith's screw drivers should always be to hand, in case your gun malfunctions. A couple of dry towels are also useful, together with a spare shooting jacket and a change of clothing if the weather really takes a turn for the worse.

6   COMPETITIONS

As well as being the sociable, friendly pastime described in Chapters 2 and 3, clay shooting is also a fiercely competitive sport. It has a full and complex structure of county, regional, national and international championships, with the Olympic Games and various World Championships at their peak.

There are two governing bodies for the sport in this country – the CPSA and the British International Board. The latter is affiliated to the International Shooting Union (ISU) and is responsible for shoots conforming to ISU rules and for those run according to rules set down by another international body – the Federation Internationale de Tir aux Armes Sportives de Chasse. Not surprisingly this is always known by its abbreviation, FITASC!

We shall deal with the different forms of clay shooting, known as disciplines, in greater detail in the next chapter, but it is worth saying here that English Sporting, English Skeet and Down-The-Line (DTL) are the basic 'domestic' disciplines, whose rules are laid down by the CPSA. There are also variations on the DTL theme, particularly Double-Rise and Handicap-by-Distance, but neither of these plays a particularly significant role on the competitive scene.

The main international disciplines are FITASC Sporting – a more complex and fiendishly difficult variation on the English Sporting theme – and ISU Skeet and Olympic Trap. The latter two are the disciplines shot at the Olympic Games, and they are generally regarded as the 'blue riband' forms of the sport.

There are also two international variations on the Trap shooting theme. These are Universal Trench, which is a simplified form of Olympic Trap, and Automatic Ball Trap (ABT) – which is a fairly unhappy sort of 'mongrel' discipline

Alan Bell receiving the award for High Gun at the DTL International –the pinnacle of achievement in this discipline.

somewhere between DTL and Olympic Trap.

All of these disciplines have their attractions, and some shooters are top quality performers at more than one of them. It is normal to specialise if you want to get to the top, however, and we'll discuss the specific requirements of each of the disciplines in the next chapter.

SPORTING

The most popular form of competitive shooting in this country is undoubtedly Sporting. You can shoot this discipline at all levels and in virtually every corner of the country – and the pinnacle awaiting those shooters who make it right to the top is the World FITASC Sporting Championship – an event in which British shooters have a record that is the envy of the world.

If you decide that Sporting is the discipline for you, simply look at any of the shooting magazines and you will find listed in their pages a tremendous variety of competitions. Indeed, if you scout through your local paper during the summer months you'll more than likely find a small 10 or 20 target shoot taking place at a country fair or fete nearby. That could be the place to take your first tentative steps.

At any of the events advertised in the shooting press, particularly if a decent prize is on offer, there will be a large number of entrants – or guns as they are known – and you are unlikely to figure in the results unless you are exceptionally talented or have been particularly well coached. Most of these events are not 'registered' with the CPSA so they are not bound by the CPSA's classification system, which does its best to ensure that shooters of similar ability compete against each other rather than in one great free-for-all.

At most of these shoots you will be able to shoot 'birds only' which means that you pay a lower entry fee than those going in for the open event – but you are not eligible for prizes even if you shoot a good score. Many of these shoots also use a re-entry system, too, whereby you can buy another card at the entry office if you are not happy with your score first time around – or if you simply want to carry on shooting!

It makes sense to join the CPSA as soon as you are relatively sure that your enthusiasm for the sport is going to last more than a few weeks. You cannot shoot in any of the major national or regional events unless you are a member – and in any case membership automatically gives you third party insurance cover up to £1 million.

Once you have joined the Association you become eligible

An Olympic Trap squad in action – note the hundreds of spent cartridge cases.

to shoot in registered events. This simply means that your score will be recorded and sent to the CPSA head office. Here they will work out your average and this will form the basis for your classification throughout the next season. In English Sporting, for example, anyone with an average over 80 per cent goes into class AA, those between 70 and 80 per cent go into class A, those between 60 and 70 per cent go into class B – and those averaging less than 60 per cent all shoot in class C. Ladies and juniors can participate in this class system, or choose to shoot in their own separate categories.

In your first full season you'll probably shoot in class B or C – and you may find that you will be able to get among the prize winners more quickly than you at first thought possible. The standard at the top of the lower classes is surprisingly high, however, but you may find that your own scores rise dramatically if you shoot a good deal in your early days.

In Sporting there is a circuit of top shoots, some of which are sponsored by various companies in or out of the gun trade – the Winchester Sporting Knock-Out for example – while others are regional championships which also serve as selection shoots for the England team. This team shoots just once a year – in the annual match against Ireland, Scotland and Wales – but the England badge is worn with pride by a number of shooters.

The two main events in this discipline, however, are the English and British Championships. The English is generally held over three days and attracts upwards of 500 guns. Like all the top shoots it is held over 100 targets – generally thrown in 10 stands – and the competition for the title is intense.

There is no doubt, however, that the British Sporting Championship is one of the biggest prizes in the sport – in fact many would say that it is the most important title on the domestic scene. Certainly the British attracts a huge number of entries – as many as 1,000 – and the man who wins it automatically becomes one of the stars of the season.

The rewards for success in Sporting shooting are greater than in any of the other disciplines – a result rather than a cause of its greater popularity. The large number of entries at events means that prize money is generally high – and also ensures that sponsors find this the most attractive of all the clay shooting disciplines.

DOWN THE LINE

Down-The-Line, or DTL as it is commonly known, is second only to Sporting in its popularity – and the overall structure of the sport is pretty similar. You can try your hand at this 'easy' form of clay shooting – and remember that easy is a relative term – at hundreds of clubs throughout the country most of which will have at least one permanent layout for this discipline.

Once again if you want to shoot in any of the major CPSA registered events you will have to become a member of the Association – and there is a similar class system, although the scores are much higher. The scoring system in DTL is three points for a first barrel kill and two points for a second barrel kill. Scores are generally written to show both the number of targets broken and the total points scored. A typical good class AA score, for example, might be 98/293 – 98 targets killed (which means six points dropped), one of them needing the second barrel (a single point dropped).

To get into class AA in DTL you need to average 94 per cent – and that is points, not just targets – so you can see that the competition at the top is pretty fierce.

Registered DTL events are almost always over 100 targets, broken into four sections of 25 targets each, but there are other ways to monitor your progress apart from the classification system. Because the layout and targets for DTL are always the same – at least in theory – you really can see how you are improving almost shoot by shoot.

The CPSA produce badges to commemorate your first 25 straight and so on up to your first 100 straight. The top DTL shooters wear jackets that are literally covered with badges!

DTL follows generally the same structure as Sporting, with regional and county championships forming a background to the main national championships. In DTL, however, there is no doubt that every shooter's main ambition is to make his or her national team for the Home International Championships – in which England, Scotland, Ireland and Wales do battle every year, taking it in turn to act as hosts.

The competition for this is intense, and outsiders to the sport would find it hard to believe the level of interest among those shooters vying for the last few places in the 25-man teams. The selection procedure varies from time to time and is different in each of the four countries – but the level of commitment remains the same.

Squads in action at the DTL International in Dublin.

The British DTL Championship is always staged at the same ground on the day following the International – so it is the only British event which rotates through the four home countries. The amount of alcohol consumed at the banquet on the night of the International can affect performances the following day!

Down-the-Line has the reputation for being boring among some shooters – generally those who have never managed to get to grips with it. It requires different shooting talents to Sporting, say, but it is still no easier to win consistently at top level.

DTL has two minor cousins – Handicap-by-Distance, which is exactly like the main discipline but with shooters standing at different distances from the trap, depending on their ability, and Double-Rise, in which two targets are thrown at once.

Neither are particularly important, but the British Double-Rise Championship is the traditional curtain-raiser to the competitive clay season, and generally provides interesting competition between specialists from different disciplines who may not see each other again for the rest of the season.

SKEET

Skeet is the last of the major domestic disciplines. It has many devotees but lacks the sheer competitive edge of DTL or the glamour and easy availability of Sporting.

Skeet shooting follows basically the same structure as the other two disciplines, with most registered shoots being over 100 targets, again shot in rounds of 25. In recent years there has even been a Home Countries International Competition introduced, with great success.

Standards at the top of English Skeet are very high indeed, with Class AA again limited to shooters with an average above 94 per cent. In fact in the British Skeet Championship for 1986, Peter Theobald had to shoot no fewer than 350 targets without a miss before he saw off all his challengers in a dramatic series of shoot-offs.

That's a record for this country – but such performances are commonplace in America, where Skeet has a tremendous following.

While it is an enjoyable competitive discipline in its own right, many shooters find Skeet rather slow. Because of the nature of the discipline, which is explained in greater detail in the next chapter, there is often a long wait between rounds. Some people like that because it gives them time to relax and socialise, while others simply get bored!

Whatever you think of Skeet as a competitive discipline there is no doubt that it is great for practice. Within a limited area, and in just 25 shots, a round of Skeet offers you just about every type of target you are likely to encounter. For a novice shooter trying to get used to different angles and to the different amounts of lead required by various targets, it is quite superb – and great fun, too.

A row of Skeet ranges at Bedford Gun Club – Britain's premier Skeet venue before running into trouble with the planners.

If you want to practise gun mounting, swinging smoothly or timing your shots correctly, Skeet offers everything you need.

THE INTERNATIONAL DISCIPLINES

Olympic Trap

Only two clay shooting disciplines are shot at the Olympic Games – Olympic Trap and ISU Skeet. It gives them a certain 'cachet' that other forms of clay shooting cannot rival, and Olympic Trap in particular is undoubtedly the 'top end' of British clay shooting. Bob Braithwaite won a gold medal for Britain in this discipline at the 1968 Olympic Games – and Olympic Trap is also the sport at which Jackie Stewart was a British Grand Prix winner long before he stood on a motor racing winner's rostrum.

The most important thing for a novice to remember is that, however easy the top shots may make it look, Olympic Trap is very hard indeed. There is probably very little point in trying your hand at this discipline competitively until you have shot at some other form of the sport at least long enough to be

Peter Croft shooting Olympic Trap. He has been European Champion at this testing discipline.

thoroughly at home with your gun and to have a good basic grasp of how to shoot clay targets! Then try a few rounds of practice before.

The competitive structure of the international disciplines is quite different to the domestic scene – largely because they are to a large extent geared towards selecting British teams to compete in European and World Championships, but also because there are relatively few shooting grounds that can stage international events at all, let alone to an acceptable standard.

This is particularly true of Olympic Trap, where there are really only half a dozen or so worthwhile grounds in the whole of Britain. The reason for this is, quite simply, that an Olympic Trap layout requires 15 traps set in a trench – the discipline is also known as Olympic Trench, in fact – as well as some pretty sophisticated electronic equipment, as described in the next chapter.

The backbone of the Olympic Trap season is provided by a number of selection shoots, all of which are held over 200 targets spread over two days. Entry fees are relatively high and the rewards are poor – so this form of shooting is really suited to those who only want the best and, to some extent, can afford to pay for it.

There are British and national Grand Prix events, also over

A Universal Trench layout at Essex Shooting Ground. Note the five automatic traps below ground.

200 targets, and a number of open, registered 100 bird shoots. Although international competition forms a natural focus for Olympic Trap, there are plenty of shooters who soon realise that they are never going to challenge for a place in the team – but who nevertheless enjoy the challenge of trying to master these very testing targets.

The classification for Olympic Trap and the other international disciplines differs slightly to that for the domestic forms of the sport, with classes A, B, C and D rather than AA, A, B and C. The average required for the top class at Olympic Trap is over 90 per cent, with the breaks for the lower classes coming at 84 and 76 per cent.

Britain has produced a number of top shooters at Olympic Trap, with Peter Croft, Peter Boden and Ian Peel all achieving major international wins in recent years. Although the Olympic Games are the most glamorous stage for the top Olympic Trap performers, there is no doubt that a win in a World, or probably even a European, Championship is harder to achieve.

Apart from the political boycotts that have weakened shooting as much as other sports at the last two Olympics, larger teams are sent to the other major championships – and with the strength in depth of countries such as Italy and Russia that makes the competition far tougher. World and European Championships are held every year – and competitors with the ability and mental toughness to stay at the top year after year are few and far between.

Once again there is a Home International Championship for Olympic Trap – but it lives very much in the shadow of the wider international scene.

Subsidiary international trap disciplines are Universal Trench – a sort of poor man's form of the Olympic discipline – and Automatic Ball Trap. Universal Trench is certainly quite popular in this country and in some European nations – but it does not have the almost universal spread of Olympic Trap.

We Brits are good at Universal Trench, however, with Peter Croft, Chris Cloke and Kevin Gill all leading the rest of Europe home in recent years. Again there are British and national Championships and selection shoots for the British team – but nearly everyone who shoots Universal Trench is actually more interested in the Olympic discipline.

Automatic Ball Trap also has the usual competitive structure, with national and British Championships and a keenly contested Home International Tournament. Its lack of sophistication compared with Olympic and Universal Trench rule it out as a really major discipline in Britain, however, and there is no major international competition overseas.

ABT is a superb practice discipline, however, and it is for this reason that it is most popular. It is far easier and cheaper to set up than either of the senior Trap disciplines and throws targets that are tough enough to hone the skills of even the best competitors.

ISU Skeet

The International form of Skeet shooting differs in several ways from its domestic counterpart – and it is very much harder. Basically the targets are speeded up and they are thrown with a delay of up to three seconds between you calling for the target and it appearing out of the trap-house.

As with Olympic Trap, ISU Skeet is shot at the Olympic Games every four years and at European and World Championships every year. Again Britain has been blessed with a

Mark Billington
shooting ISU Skeet
for Great Britain.

number of top class competitors in recent years, with Joe Neville, Paul Bentley and Ken Harman being just three from a large group of consistent high scorers.

As with Olympic Trap there are relatively few grounds where you can shoot ISU Skeet. In all clay shooting disciplines shooters not unreasonably demand that the targets should conform to the regulations – but that is particularly the case with ISU Skeet. The top performers are particularly quick to condemn grounds that don't meet the required standard – and this coupled with the fact that ISU Skeet is a relatively low 'earner' from a ground's point of view means that many of them are reluctant to stage the discipline at all. Far easier to stick to the easier to run and more popular domestic version of the discipline.

Once again the season is built around the selection shoots for the British team, as well as the British and English Championships. All major competitions are over 200 targets and two days – and it has to be admitted that ISU Skeet is a discipline that requires exceptional dedication and persistence.

FITASC Sporting
If there is one international discipline in which the British truly excel it is FITASC Sporting. Performers such as Brian Hebditch, Paddy Howe, Brian Wells, A.J. Smith and Barry Simpson – and there are others, too – have ruled the roost in Europe and the world for ten years and more, with only occasional interventions from particularly talented Frenchmen and Belgians.

As with the other international disciplines there are World and European Championships every year – although part of the reason for the British dominance of this sport is that it only has a really strong following in France, Belgium, Spain and, to a lesser extent, Germany, Switzerland, Australia and South Africa. Interest is growing in the rest of the world, however – particularly in the USA – and the intensity of competition is increasing.

There are selection shoots for the British team in the World and European Championships, but they do not have the same importance as in Skeet and Trap because individuals can and do enter for these championships in their own right. In fact there will generally be dozens of British shooters at either of the major international championships.

FITASC Sporting, by its nature, is relatively expensive to set up and slow to shoot – with the result that grounds have to charge high entry fees merely to cover their costs. It is unlikely to ever replace the domestic form of the sport in popularity – but its difficulty and the variety of targets makes it the discipline which virtually every shooter enjoys and respects.

There probably is not a great deal of point in trying your hand at FITASC until you have pretty well mastered the domestic discipline, but it is a fascinating form of the sport – and the top shoots often take places in areas of great natural beauty, which adds to the pleasure.

Star Shot

Finally to the discipline which is the most recent on the scene and still the rarest – although it is probably familiar to more of the general public than any other form of clay shooting. Star Shot is a discipline that was purpose built for television, and it produced highly entertaining viewing in its pilot series at the end of 1986 and in the first full series in 1987 .

There are a few grounds which have Star Shot layouts, where you can discover that it is very much harder than the

Duncan Lawton shooting FITASC Sporting. He is the only top Sporting shot to use a semi-automatic shotgun.

top shots make it appear on television. It is too soon to say whether this discipline will catch on competitively, but certainly there is no general competitive framework for it at the moment.

It is fun, though – and that is what clay shooting is really all about.

Star Shot is an exciting new form of clay shooting specially developed for television. Here you can see a clay target being broken by A.J. Smith.

7 DISCIPLINES

Discipline is a dirty word to some – and the be-all and end-all to others. In clay shooting, though, it is simply the word that refers to the different forms of the sport. In short, each discipline is really just a set of rules and regulations.

We have already referred to the various disciplines in previous chapters, but now we will outline the precise rules for each of them as simply as possible and also point out the various attractions of each of the different disciplines. We will also mention the guns and cartridges that are generally considered suitable for each, and some basic shooting methods. In no way will we attempt to provide a coaching manual, however, as that lies beyond the scope of this book. However, the books listed at the end of the book may provide useful further reading.

Before considering each discipline in turn, let us just

Different types of clay target. Left to right: Mini, midi, standard, rabbit, battue.

Clay targets stacked up and ready to use.

outline some basic rules that apply to all of them. For a start, any shotgun may be used provided it is no bigger than 12 bore. Cartridges must have a maximum shot load weight of 1⅛ oz, with the exception of FITASC Sporting, where the maximum limit is 1¼ oz. Shot sizes between 6 and 9 are allowed, although in fact only the most eccentric shooters would use anything larger than size 7. Now let's turn to each of the disciplines.

ENGLISH SPORTING

By its nature, Sporting is the least disciplined form of clay shooting. In recent years English Sporting has followed the FITASC variant by allowing the use of many different types of clay target in addition to the conventional type. These are the 'midi' – smaller than standard, so faster off the trap arm and a little more difficult to see; the 'mini' – smaller still and very hard to see if thrown a long way from the shooter or against a difficult background; the 'battue' – a much flatter target which flies very fast, is hard to break and which tends to curve as it slows down; and the 'rabbit' – a large, flat edged target which is intended to be rolled along the ground but which is also sometimes used through the air.

The use of these different types of target has increased still further the variety of shots which you may encounter on a typical Sporting shoot. Even the most experienced shooters can sometimes be fooled into thinking that a midi thrown quite close and relatively slowly, for example, is a standard sized target thrown at great height and speed. Make that sort of mistake and you are unlikely to make contact!

The universal appeal of Sporting

Sporting shoots are divided into stands – generally ten stands or more with ten targets on each for a 100 target shoot, but possibly six stands with five targets on each for a 30-bird shoot, say.

On each stand these targets may be thrown as singles – which means what it says – as simultaneous doubles, as 'trailing' doubles or as doubles 'on report'. A simultaneous double is simply one in which the targets are thrown at the same time. A trailing double is one in which the trapper throws the first target and then follows it with the second as soon as he can cock, load and release the trap. An 'on report' double is one in which the second target is released when the trapper hears the report of the shooter's attempt to hit the first target.

It will become obvious once you start shooting that pairs of targets which are 'killable' as a pair on report would be impossible if thrown as a simultaneous pair. The art of a good shoot organiser lies in providing a good variety of targets, with something relatively easy for the novice to hit but also other stands which sort the men out from the boys.

At some shoots you will come across stands where organisers have the clays thrown so far away that they are almost impossible to hit because they are out of range, or against such difficult backgrounds that they are almost impossible to see! Such devices are neither necessary nor popular. It is quite possible to set out a course that will test the best simply by subtle use of terrain, speed and angle.

Key terms that you will hear on visiting a Sporting shoot are 'finding the birds', 'getting the right picture', and 'lead'.

Trappers in a Sporting shoot should be protected from flying shot and pieces of broken clay by straw bales.

Lead basically refers to the amount of space which you have to shoot in front of a target in order to hit it. The actual distance is a matter of fact – and can be measured more or less if you know the speed, trajectory and distance of the target and the speed, trajectory and distance of your shot load. Stated simply the shot load takes a certain amount of time to travel the 35 yards or so to the target. During that time the target will also have moved, so if you were 'aiming' at the target when you pulled the trigger you will miss it behind.

While this may be a fact, what you actually see when you pull a trigger and break a target may be very different to what someone else 'sees' when he does the same. Some shooters will say that they have given a far distant target a barn door and half lead, while others will say that they simply swung through the target fast and pulled the trigger as the muzzles passed it. Both are correct, of course, but they have a different sight picture. The key thing with any Sporting target is to concentrate on what you are doing and remember what you saw when you break any given target. Repeat that every time and, all things being equal, you should break the target every time. It is much harder than it sounds!

'Finding the birds' has nothing to do with the relative scarcity of females at Sporting shoots! Rather it refers to the process by which Sporting shooters establish the correct sight picture of any given target.

On seeing a stand for the first time you make your own assessment of where you will try to shoot it – and you may well have watched other shooters on that stand to help you form a view. Hopefully you will find them first time – but it could be that you miss with your first attempt and therefore have to make some adjustment for your second try. You might increase or decrease your lead, for example.

There is no real substitute for experience when it comes to finding the birds – but even the most experienced shooters can still become totally confused at times. One of our top shooters missed out on a good chance of winning the British Open Sporting Championship in 1986 when he simply could not find the birds on his last stand, the High Tower. He hit the first five as sweetly as you could ask – but then missed the sixth. He thought he had missed it behind and pulled further in front next time. Still he missed the seventh and eighth, so he pulled yet further in front for targets nine and ten – both of which sailed past. His only conclusion could be that he had missed that sixth target in front – but his failure to 'find the birds' again put him right out of contention.

Finally, before moving to a consideration of the basic types of Sporting stand, a few words about the guns required and about basic shooting technique.

The first point to remember, and one that will be hammered into you if you go to a shooting school, is that you do not aim a shotgun – you point it. Your eyes should always be focussed on the target, not on the rib, which you should be aware of only peripherally. And a shotgun should always be on the move – as in so many other sports it is essential that you follow through with your swing. If you stop when you pull the trigger – and it is all too natural to do so – you will miss your target.

In recent years the Sporting rules have been changed so that you can shoot 'gun up' – which simply means that you can call for the target with the gun already mounted into your shoulder. This was introduced largely because it was becoming difficult for inexperienced referees to police the previous rule which insisted that the gun should be out of the shoulder when you called for the target.

In fact you will see relatively few shooters taking advantage of the 'gun up' rule. Most find it encourages greater smoothness and a more natural technique to have the gun out of the shoulder when they call for the targets – and it is also a general rule that you should 'ease' the gun between shots when taking a double. A hold favoured by many shooters is to tuck the butt just under the armpit when in the 'ready' position. This means that you know exactly where the gun is, and also makes it natural to mount the gun correctly into the 'pocket' inside your shoulder, rather than out on the shoulder muscle itself.

Sporting stands can come in an almost infinite variety of forms. Traditionally they have been named after various types of live quarry – driven grouse, high pheasant and so on – but this habit is now dying out as the sport grows ever further away from its live quarry shooting roots.

In Sporting these days you may come across targets thrown in just about any way and at any range provided it is safe – so it follows that you need a good all-round gun. Until a few years ago many shooters took two or three guns with them on a Sporting shoot – a Trap gun for long range targets, a Skeet gun for close targets and a game gun for the rest.

With the advent of screw-in chokes, however, and with a greater awareness of how to influence pattern spread by choice of cartridges, the need for your own personal arsenal has disappeared. Most gun ranges include a Sporting model, which will generally be of medium weight – between 7 and 8 lbs – with barrels of 28 or 30 inches. Most will be available with screw-in chokes, but if you don't like these you'll find that a choking of ¼ and ½ in a gun with a single selective trigger will enable you to cope with most of the stands you find.

Cartridges are generally a mixture of Trap and Skeet versions, with some companies now producing a range of cartridges carrying the Sporting tag, too.

Perhaps the best way to illustrate the variety of stands on a Sporting course is to take you around an imaginary 10 stand, 100 target layout. Remember that you are free to walk around the layout as much as you like before shooting it, and that in 99 per cent of events you can take the stands in any order you like.

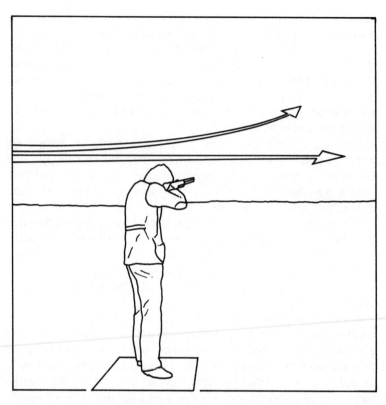

Stand 1 A pair of left to right crossers, with the further target also travelling slightly away from you, thrown simultaneously. Watch the other guns to see which target they shoot first – and remember that if you miss with your first shot you'll probably do as well to use the second barrel on the same target, rather than trying to catch the other one.

Stand 2 Two targets from behind your head on report. The first comes directly overhead, not too high, the second drifts out to the left, very slowly. This sort of target is easy to miss in front and above.

Stand 3 A typical 'grouse' stand. Targets thrown fast and low virtually straight towards you. There are endless variations of angle possible here.

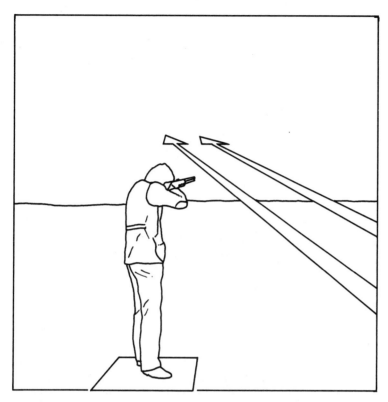

Stand 4 A pair of targets thrown from your right and behind you, quartering away to your left in front of you, fast and low. The organiser may make these midis if he really wants to get you on your toes.

Stand 5 A pair of targets from a medium height tower. A normal target straight overhead, followed on report by a screaming mini out to the left. Blink and you'll miss it!

Stand 6 A type of stand that is becoming more common. You stand looking down into a gulley, along which a pair of 'trailing' orange clays are thrown.

Stand 7 A rabbit clay bounces along in front of you from right to left, followed on report by a quartering midi, also from right to left, and difficult to 'read' against a sloping background.

Stand 8 A typical 'teal' stand. Two targets thrown from 25 yards in front of you and virtually straight up in the air. Generally reckoned to be a 'gift' by the top shots – and many are missed as a result!

Stand 9 A midi from your left, moving straight away from you fast into the air. Followed on report by a normal clay flopping slowly towards you.

Stand 10 The high tower. A 'trailing' pair of midis thrown high and fast. They should be relatively straightforward against the perfect background of the sky – but the high tower has its own mystique and very few shooters like them.

FITASC Sporting

The general rules about guns apply for FITASC, where you are only allowed one gun for the whole shoot. Typically a FITASC shoot consists of 150 targets, each split into 25 target layouts. You shoot in a squad of six, taking it in turns as to who shoots first on the various 'stands' within each layout.

As we have said earlier, this is probably the toughest discipline there is – and you are unlikely to try it unless you have shot a fair amount of English Sporting first.

Down the line

As shown in the diagram DTL has five shooting positions situated in an arc 16 yards behind the trap. You shoot in a five man squad, taking the targets in turn one at a time, moving to the next stand to the right after each five targets.

Like all the Trap disciplines, DTL is shot 'gun-up' already mounted in your shoulder. Once you are set – relaxed, with the gun correctly in your shoulder, your cheek on the stock and your aiming eye looking straight down the rib – you should switch the focus of your eyes to the area just above and in front of the traphouse where you will first be able to pick up the target. It is important not to let your eye focus on the rib, as can easily happen in the gun-up disciplines. As soon as you are ready, call for the target and shoot it – hopefully with the first barrel, remember, because you lose points in DTL for a second barrel kill.

Different shooters aim their guns at different points while waiting for the target to appear. Basically the choices are between above the traphouse or at the top of the traphouse, and, laterally, between the centre of the traphouse and some point to the side of that line depending which stand you are on.

At this stage, as a novice, it is probably easiest to start by taking the dead centre position, experimenting with others as you become more proficient or under the guidance of a coach.

On the DTL circuit you will also see a wide variety of stances, from a 'natural' threequarter-on stance to a much more square-on, less comfortable position. Similarly you'll see all manner of arm positions from the dramatic elbows in the air approach to a conventional relaxed position.

There are successful practitioners of just about every DTL method and technique, and every individual reading this book will no doubt develop their own. The basics to remember are to adopt a position that feels comfortable – and which does not seem to inhibit your movement for any of the targets.

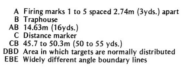

A Firing marks 1 to 5 spaced 2.74m (3yds.) apart
B Traphouse
AB 14.63m (16yds.)
C Distance marker
CB 45.7 to 50.3m (50 to 55 yds.)
DBD Area in which targets are normally distributed
EBE Widely different angle boundary lines

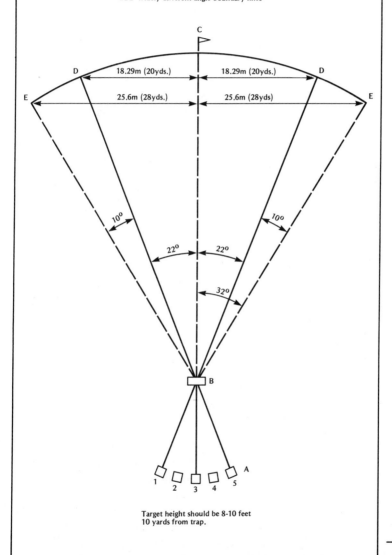

Target height should be 8-10 feet
10 yards from trap.

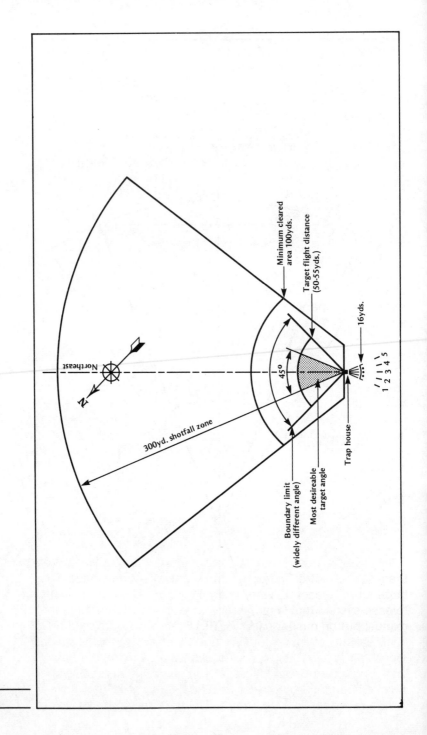

Minimum cleared area 100yds.

Target flight distance (50-55yds.)

16yds.

1 2 3 4 5

Northeast

N

45°

300yd. shotfall zone

Boundary limit (widely different angle)

Most desireable target angle

Trap house

Most shooters use a conventional Trap gun for DTL, often choked very tightly at half and full or even full and full. It is doubtful whether such tight chokes are necessary or even desirable. DTL targets have a maximum travel of 50-55 yards, so they are relatively slow and you should be able to kill them comfortably enough with modern Trap cartridges and half choke.

A gun designed for DTL will have 30 or 32 inch barrels, a non-selective single trigger – because you always shoot the more open choked bottom barrel first – and a relatively high stock. The latter enables you to shoot the targets, all of which rise at the same angle, as shown in the diagram, while keeping them in view above the rib. This is clearly a great advantage, particularly for second barrel shots. Automatics are not favoured for Trap shooting, incidentally, because their ejection of spent cartridges in front of the next shooter is off-putting.

All the major cartridge makers produce two or three varieties of Trap cartridge. For DTL there is no point in using the more expensive 'super grade' varieties developed for Olympic Trap, and any normal brand should no the job. Experiment with different types to find the combination of speed and recoil that suits you best.

Olympic trap

At first glance Olympic Trap can look very much like a 'souped up' kind of DTL. In fact, however, there are so many differences between the two that a DTL shooter taking on Olympic Trap for the first time is probably at no great advantage over any other shooter, except that he will be used to shooting gun-up.

The targets in Olympic Trap are a lot faster than in DTL, with a greater variety of angles allowed, and a variation in height, too. They also differ slightly in speed, whereas DTL targets are all thrown the same, and you shoot just one target from each of the five stands before moving on to the next one.

An Olympic Trap layout has five banks of three traps, each of them set 16 metres in front of one of the shooting stands. The targets are released immediately on your call by an acoustic release system that is far faster and more consistent than the manual button pusher used in DTL. Sophisticated electronics ensures that every shooter in an Olympic Trap competition receives the same targets – although the variations are such that you don't know which target you are going to receive and when. Experienced shots can 'read' a layout so that they have a fair idea what to expect for their last few targets – but most would

A typical Olympic Trap squad in action.

admit that they probably miss as many targets through getting this wrong as they gain through getting it right.

Because of the degree of swing necessary for the wide angle Trap targets, virtually all the top shooters favour a narrow stance, with the feet close together and threequarters on to the traps. Comments regarding hold position and eye focus are much as for DTL, although very few Olympic Trap shooters favour a hold position with the muzzle pointing right at the top of the trap house.

Many shooters would use the same gun for DTL and Olympic Trap, although the demands made by the discipline are very different. Chokes will need to be tighter, because of the great speed and distance of the targets, and the most open chokes you'll find will be half and full, with most shooters opting for threequarters and full or full and full.

Barrel lengths will be 30 or 32 inches, with the latter much favoured recently. Trap guns are generally relatively heavy, to absorb recoil, and an Olympic Trap gun will have a high stock – although probably not quite so high as a specialist DTL gun because of the relatively low targets mixed with the high ones in Olympic Trap.

Cartridges are just as for DTL, although many manufacturers produce special high grade cartridges to give tighter patterns and high velocity for the longer range targets. You have to pay extra for this superior quality, of course, but very many Olympic

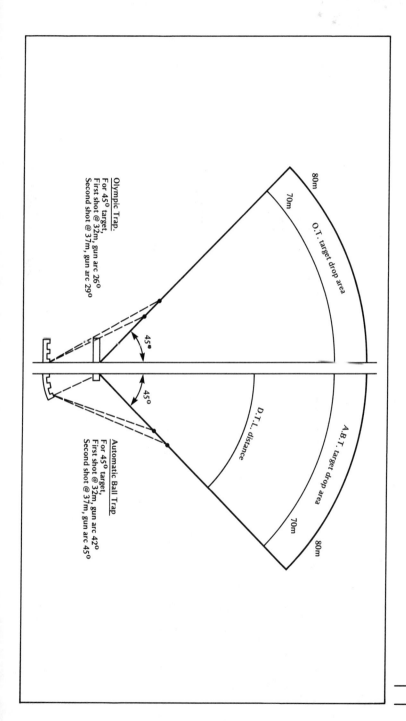

Olympic Trap.
For 45° target,
First shot @ 32m, gun arc 26°
Second shot @ 37m, gun arc 29°

80m
70m
O.T. target drop area

45°

45°

D.T.L. distance

A.B.T. target drop area

70m
80m

Automatic Ball Trap
For 45° target,
First shot @ 32m, gun arc 42°
Second shot @ 37m, gun arc 45°

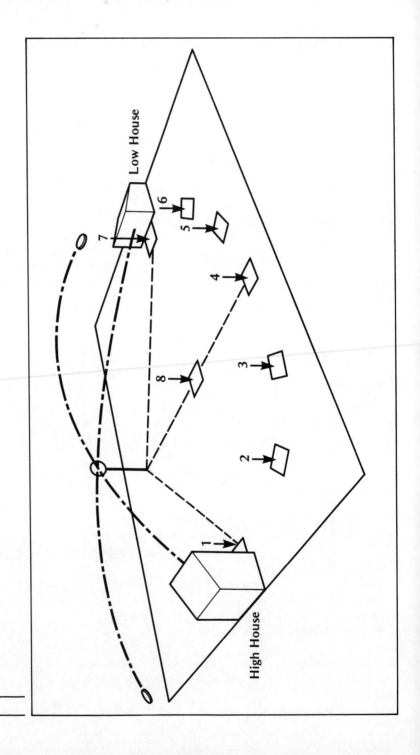

Low House

High House

Trap shooters use a better, more expensive cartridge in their second barrel.

You shoot Olympic Trap in squads of six, moving from stand to stand after each shot. Each 25 target round begins with the shooter on stand one taking his first target. When he has shot the second man shoots. He moves on, is replaced by the shooter from stand 1, whose place in turn is taken by the shooter who was standing 'spare' at the start of the round.

Universal trench and ABT.

The layouts for Universal Trench and ABT are as shown in the diagrams. As with Olympic Trap, Universal Trench is 'computerised' to give all shooters an equal chance throughout the event. In ABT this is not the case and it is possible for one shooter to be faced with a high proportion of extreme angle and height 'screamers', while another has a large proportion of relatively easy targets.

The general rules for gun, ammunition, stance and technique are as for Olympic Trap.

English skeet

A Skeet layout is as shown in the diagram, with the targets thrown on fixed trajectories and speeds from the high and low towers on either side of the layout. The shooters move from station to station, starting at station 1, taking the targets prescribed in the rules one by one. These are described below – and you'll see that they add up to only 24, rather than 25. In fact if you shoot these 24 targets 'straight' you are then given the option of taking either the high or low target on station 7 again to make up your 25.

If you miss a target on any of the stations you are given that one again to make up the 25. This applies to your first miss only, of course. Any further mistakes simply come off your score and you carry on through the round.

The targets from each station are as follows:

Station 1 High house single, low house single, double (high first).

Station 2 High house single, low house single, double (high first).

Station 3 High house single, low house single.

Station 4 High house single, low house single, double (either first).

Station 5 High house single, low house single.

Skeet targets have to pass through this hoop in order to conform to regulations.

Station 6 High house single, low house single, double (low first).

Station 7 High house single, low house single, double (low first).

While English Skeet is a popular discipline it has relatively few shooters who shoot it and nothing else. Many people shoot this discipline quite happily with their normal Sporting gun, fitted with open chokes if it is a multichoke, or even with a Trap gun.

Purpose built Skeet guns are common, however, and are considered virtually essential for the international form of the discipline.

Because all the targets have to be shot at relatively close range in Skeet open chokes are required together with cartridges using size 9 shot and designed to give a relatively wide spread. There was a fashion a few years ago for very short barrels – 26 inches – but the current trend is for barrels around 28 inches long, and some shooters even favour 30 inch barrels.

English Skeet targets are relatively slow – they are set to travel 55 yards – so you do not need a fast handling gun. Weight

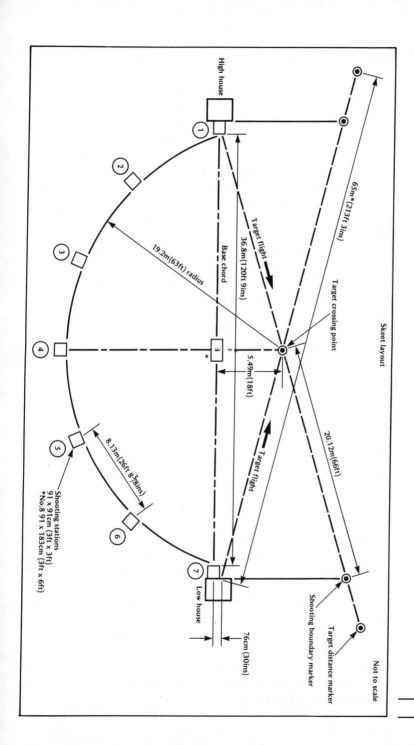

Skeet layout

High house

① ② ③ ④ ⑤ ⑥ ⑦

Low house

65m*(213ft 3ins)

Target crossing point

20.12m(66ft)

Target flight
36.8m(120ft 9ins)

19.2m(63ft) radius

Base chord

5.49m(18ft)

*3

Target flight

8.13m(26ft 8⅜ins)

Shooting stations
91 x 91cm (3ft x 3ft)
*No.8 91 x 183cm (3ft x 6ft)

76cm (30ins)

Shooting boundary marker

Target distance marker

Not to scale

97

will tend to be over 7½ lbs, therefore, and the stock dimensions will be designed to give a flat shooting gun – so that it shoots exactly where you point it.

Gun position for English Skeet is optional, and many shooters now shoot 'gun-up'. If you are used to shooting gun-down, however, you'll do as well to continue doing so in Skeet. Target release is instantaneous and you should focus your eyes in a position where you will first be able to see the targets. From most of the stations that will mean just in front of the trap house opening – although you would obviously need a double-jointed neck to do that for the high target on station 1, for example!

ISU skeet

While the Skeet layout itself is exactly the same as for English Skeet, the two disciplines are actually quite different. For a start a very pronounced gun down position is written into the rules, and you must call for the targets with your gun stock touching your hip bone. The targets are thrown faster – to a range of 72 yards – and there is a random delay of up to three seconds between your calling for the target and it appearing.

The target pattern for ISU Skeet is as follows:

Station 1 High house single, double (high first).

Station 2 High house single, low house single, double (high first).

Station 3 High house single, low house single, double (high first).

Station 4 High house single, low house single.

Station 5 High house single, low house single, double (low first).

Station 6 High house single, low house single, double (low first.

Station 7 Double (low first).

Station 8 High house single, low house single.

You'll notice here that ISU Skeet involves the use of station 8 for a pair of very fast, close range singles. These are generally reckoned to be next to impossible by novices, but it is very rare for any experienced Skeet shooter to miss them – and the trick really is to see the targets early and pull the trigger as soon as you have mounted your gun.

For most types of shooting we have assumed the use of some variation of the 'swing through' form of shooting. This assumes that you start with the gun's muzzles behind the target and then swing it through on the right line, timing your release of the shot to break the target.

ISU Skeet, however, allows a different style which has found much favour with many shooters. It is called the 'maintained lead' method and is made possible by the fact the Skeet targets always follow the same path and travel at the same speed. It is equally applicable to the domestic form of the discipline, although not so commonly used.

As the name implies, this system means that you always keep the muzzles out in front of the target, and the main advantage of this system is that it allows you to take the targets earlier. This is a particular advantage on the doubles, where the relatively fast targets can get away from you using more conventional methods.

A purpose built Skeet gun is essential for ISU, with special Skeet chokes to give wide patterns at close range, and a stock designed for smooth and easy mounting. Cartridges are size 9, generally producing pretty high velocities.

Star shot

The Star Shot layout consists of a metal arc split into four segments, and each of these is then split into three sections. Each segment has its own trap, and these get faster as you move from left to right. Each section is numbered, with one being the top left section and 12 the bottom right – and you have to be very quick indeed to hit the section 12 target with any consistency.

It is very early days for Star Shot, but already 'special' guns have been developed. These basically have very short barrels, to give very fast handling, and open chokes. The top shooters have also developed some slightly unconventional techniques, involving degrees of cant that any novice would be unwise to copy.

LEADING GROUNDS

West London SG (01-845 1377). Another famous shooting ground that has been patronised by members of the Royal Family. Coaching facilities are excellent, but again prices will be high.

Mid-Norfolk SS (0603 860436). Arguably the best Sporting ground in the country, with excellent coaching available at moderate prices. Also facilities for Skeet and Trap.

Northampton GC (078887 650). One of the best presented grounds in the country, with excellent facilities for Skeet, Sporting and Trap. Good coaching and reasonable prices.

Bywell SG (0661 25885). Now recognised as the top DTL and ABT ground in the country, Bywell offers excellent competitive and practice facilities.

West Midland SG (093924 644). An attractive and well laid out ground, with excellent Sporting facilities, plus Skeet and DTL. The ground is distinguished by its huge 'log cabin' clubhouse.

Garland's SG (082785 216). Like North Wales SS, Garland's offers superb facilities for all kinds of Trap shooting. Similarly it is also a good place to buy a gun and cartridges at competitive prices, and to be able to try it out on the ranges.

North Wales Shooting School (0244 81 22 19). Over the years this has become recognised as the premier Trap shooting ground in the country, with layouts for Olympic Trap, Skeet, DTL and ABT. It is the traditional home of the British Olympic Trap Grand Prix, and is open daily for practice, coaching or competitions.

Blandford & Dorchester GC (093583 625). One of the best equipped grounds in the country, with extensive layouts for Sporting, Skeet and Trap.

Kingsferry GC (0795 872953). The most popular and well respected Skeet ground in the country, which has become the home of the British Skeet Championship in recent years.

Leicestershire WA (0536 203626 (day) or 053753 2007). This centrally located ground has facilities for Skeet, Sporting, DTL and ABT, plus good coaching by appointment.

Holland & Holland SS (09274 25349). Owned by one of London's top gun-makers, the ground has excellent facilities for Sporting, plus Skeet and ABT.

CLAY CLUB GUIDE

AVON
Avon SG, Stowey Quarry, Bishop Sutton, near Bristol. Tel: 0761 52356.
Monument SG, Hawkesbury Upton near Badminton, Avon. Tel: 0454 310919.
BEDFORDSHIRE
Flitwick GC, Folly Farm, Maulden Road, Flitwick, Beds. Tel: 0525 713099.
Gransden SG, Gransden Airfield, Gread Gransden, Sandy, Beds. Tel: 0767 27663.
BERKSHIRE
Flower Pot CPC, Flower Pot, Alston, Henley-on-Thames, Berks, Tel: 0628 33480.
Thames Valley Sg, Tomb Farm, Upper Basildon, near Pangbourne, Berks. Tel: 049162 703.
BUCKINGHAMSHIRE
South Bucks SC, Honor End Lane, Prestwood, Great Missenden, Bucks. Tel: 0494 774705.
Valley View ISGC, on A413, near Little Missenden, between Amersham & Great Missenden. Tel: 0442 54736.
Woodlands Farm GC, Woodlands Farm, Weston Underwood, near Olney. Tel: 0908 606950.
CAMBRIDGESHIRE
Fenland GC, Mepal Airport, near Sutton Ely, Cambs. Tel: 0354 53290.
Greenend Sg, Primrose Hall, Three Holes, Wisbech, Cambs. Tel: 03548 335..
Hinxton SG, on A1301 between A11 and A505, about five miles south of Cambridge. Tel: 0223 844001.
Pye GC, Denny Abbey Farm, Waterbeach, near Cambridge. Tel:

0223 61222.
CHESHIRE
Blakelow CSC, Higher Blakelow Farm, off A537, Macclesfield, Cheshire. Tel: 0625 32191.
Croughton SG, Top Farm, Croughton, near Chester. Tel: 0244 381104.
Holmes Chapel SG, Primrose Farm, Sproston, Holmes Chapel, Crewe, Cheshire. Tel: 0477 32165.
Little Mill SG, Rowarth, Stockport, Cheshire. Tel: 0663 43273.
Lyme SG, Mudhurst Lane, Disley, near Stockport, Tel: 061-368 1871.
North Wales SS, Manor Farm, Sealand, near Chester. Tel: 0244 812219.
CLEVELAND
Cleveland GC, Stanghow, off A171, Guisborough. Tel: 0287 43865.
Cleveland Potash CPSC, Boulby Mine, Loftus, Cleveland. Tel: 0287 40140 ext 221.
Wynyard Park SG, Wolviston, Billingham, Cleveland. Tel: 0642 554996.
CORNWALL
Camelford & DGC, Helsbury Quarry, Michaelstow, near Camelford, Cornwall. Tel: 0840 212703/ 212512.
Cornwall GC, off A30, three miles west of Zelah, Cornwall. Tel: 087252 514.
County GC, Lower Lake SG, Upton Cross, Liskeard, Cornwall. Tel: 0579 62319.
Mount Hawke, Mingoose, Porthtown, Redruth, Cornwall. Tel: 0736 66824.
West Cornwall SG, Cucurrian Farm, Ludgvan, Penzance, Cornwall. Tel: 0736 740275.

West Penwith GC, St Erth, Hayle, Cornwall. Tel: 0736 850802.

CUMBRIA

Carlisle & DGC, White Heather Hotel, Kirkbride Airfield, Kirkbride, Cumbria. Tel: 0965 44198.

Cockermouth & DGC, Rowrah, near Frizington, West Cumbria. Tel: 0900 822501.

Duddon Valley GC, Broughton Mills, between Broughton-in-Furness & Coniston. Tel: 0229 64234/52029.

Penrith & DGC, Bowscar, Penrith, Cumbria. Tel: 0768 62256.

DERBYSHIRE

Buxton S & TC, Dove Holes SG, Dale Road, Dove Holes, Buxton. Tel: 061483 0301/7414.

Charcon GC, Charcon Works, Hulland Ward, off A517, near Derby. Tel: 0332 831759.

Cold Springs GC (Derbys). On A5002, 1 mile north of Buxton. Tel: 0298 5584.

Dale CPC, The Windmill, Cat & Fiddle Lane, Dale Abbey, Derbys. Tel: 0602 326198.

Hayfield GC, above Sportsman Inn, Kinder Rd, Hayfield, Berbys. Tel: 06632 2312.

Mapperley SC, Glovers Farm, off A609, Mapperley. Tel: 0602 753169.

Melbourne GC, off B587, Melbourne, Derbys. Tel: 03316 2834.

Ockbrook GC, Ashton-on-Trent, Derby. Tel: 0332 761673.

Quarnford SG, Upper Drystone Edge, Quarnford, near Buxton. Tel: 0298 2204.

Springwood SG, between Milton and Ingleby, near Burton on Trent. Tel: 03316 2834.

Yeaveley SG, Yeaveley, Ashbourne, Derbys. Tel: 033523 247.

DEVON

Devon & Exeter GC, Thorns Cross, on A380 between Exeter and Newton Abbot. Tel: 039 285 602.

North Devon GC, Tower Field, Tawstock, nr. Barnstaple, Devon. Tel: 0271 870229/813604.

Sheldon CS, Southcott Farm, Sheldon, near Honiton. Tel: 0404 84276/2651.

DORSET

Blandford & Dorchester GC, Clay Pigeon Restaurant, Wardon Hill, A37, Dorchester, Dorset. Tel: 093583 625.

DURHAM

Butterknowle GC, Wilton Castle, Wilton-le-Wear, Bishop Auckland, Co. Durham. Tel: 0325 317657.

Woodlands Close GC, Woodlands Close Farm, Spencers Moor, Station Rown, Co. Durham. Tel: 0429 61127.

ESSEX

Essex SG, near Fyfield Hall, Ongar Essex. Tel: 0992 718296.

Fisher Reeves SG, Hall Farm, Little Bardfield, near Braintree, Essex. Tel: 037 810652.

Hoggs Farm CC, Hoggs Farm, Harlow Common, Harlow. Tel: 0279 925803/37915.

Ingrebourne GC, White Bear Inn, London Road, Stanford Rivers, near Ongar, Essex. Tel: 037881 2586.

Maryland & DGC, Brook Hall Farm, Bradwell-Steeple Road, Latchingdon, Essex. Tel: 0268 781241.

Newland Hall GC, Neland Hall, Roxwell, near Chelmsford, Essex. Tel: 0245 31463.

Old Park Bores SG, The Poultry Farm, Old Mead Rd, Elsenham, Essex. Tel: 0371 820987.

Shooters Wharf GC, KT House, Stanhope Ind. Park, Wharf Road, Stanford-le-Hope, Essex.

South East Essex GC, Pickerels Farm, Watery Lane, near Battles-bridge, Essex. Tel: 0277 233468.

GLOUCESTERSHIRE

Fodarm CPC, The Trout Farm, Stow St Briavels, Coleford, Glos. Tel: 0594 33908.

Gloucester CSC, opposite King's Head Inn, Norton on A38, Glos. Tel: 0452 415637.

Lydney CPSC, Woolaston Station, near Lydney, Gloucester. Tel: 05944 2607.

Stroud & DGC, Water Lane, Bisley, Gloucester. Tel: 04536 70420/5779.

HAMPSHIRE

Avon Valley GC, Chatsworth Sandpit, next to Blue Haze Kennels, off B3081. Tel: 0425 615053.

Brockenhurst GC, New Park Farm Equestrian Centre, Brockenhurst, New Forest, Hants. Tel: 0425

620459.
Cadnam GC, Cadnam Lane,
Newbridge, Hants. Tel: 042127
2628.
Fareham GC, Titchfield Lane,
Fontley, near Fareham, Hants. Tel:
0329 662347/0329 832335.
Gosport & Fareham SGC, Cherque
Farm, Shoot Lane, off Lee-on-Solent
Road, Hants. Tel: 0329 286084.
Herriard SG, Lee Farm or Lasham
Woods, A339 between Basingstoke
and Alton, Hants. Tel: 025 683 277
(day)/0420 84441 (evenings).
Long Sutton GC, off A32, Long
Sutton, near Odiham, Hants. Tel:
0420 83064.
Test Valley CPC, Freemantle Park
Farm, Hannington, near Basingstoke,
Hants. Tel: 0256 770872 (day).
HEREFORD
Hereford GC, Haywood, A49, near
Hereford. Tel: 0432 267571.
Symonds Cider GC, A465
Hereford-Bromyard Road, Tel:
09817 7519.
HERTFORDSHIRE
Broomhills GC, Hicks Road,
Maryate, St Albans, Herts. Tel: 0582
64649.
Colliers End GC, Silkmead Farm,
north of Hare Street, on B1368,
Herts. Tel: 0279 724681.
Lea Valley SG, Bramfield Rd, off
A602, Hertford, Tel: 0992 59212.
Little Amwell GC, Townsend Arms,
Hertford Heath, Herts. Tel: 0992
57428/58630.
HUMBERSIDE
Ancholme Valley SG, B1205,
Kirton-in-Lindsey Airfield, South
Humberside. Tel: 0777 818362.
Holme-on-Spalding Moor CPC,
Howden Road, Holme-on-Spalding
Moor, North Humberside. Tel: 0696
60805.
Humberside SG, Catwick Lane,
Brandesburton, North Humberside.
Tel: 0482 445284.
ISLE OF MAN
Ayre CPC, Blue Point, Andreas, Isle
of Man. Tel: 0624 88374.
ISLE OF WIGHT
Isle of Wight GC, Sainham, Godshill
(Sporting)/Newton Range, Porchfield
Newport (DTL). Tel: 0983 527132.
Shepherds Chine SG, Compton

Fields Farm, Atherfield Bay, near
Chale, Isle of Wight. Tel: 0983
740074 (eve).
KENT
Bourne Wood SG, Sheepcote
Lane, Swanley, Kent. Tel: 04747
5180/0322 21576.
Bunters Hill GC, Blacklands Farm,
Higham Road, Wainscott, near
Rochester, Kent. Tel: 0634 716471.
Charing GC, Charing Hill, off A252
Charing-Canterbury Road, Kent. Tel:
023371 2978.
Kent GC, School Lane, Horton
Kirby, near Dartford, Kent. Tel: 0732
822475.
Kent WA, Detling Showground,
Detling, Kent. Tel: 0322 524255.
Kingsferry GC, Old Ferry Road, off
A249, Isle of Sheppey. Tel: 0795
872953.
Robin Hood GC, White Hills SG,
Exedown Road, Ightham, off A20,
Kent. Tel: 0732 823611.
West Kent SS, Elm Court Estate,
Lidsing, Chatham, Kent. Tel: 0622
813230.
Westwood & Castle Hill GC,
Westwood Farm, Weald, Kent. Tel:
0883 45104.
Windmill CS, Hoo, off A228 Isle of
Grain Road. Tel: 0634 250254.
Woodchurch GC, Boulder Wall
Farm, off Dungeness Road, Lydd,
Romney Marsh, Kent. Tel: 0797
222144.
Woodland GC, Upper Austin Lodge
Farm, Upper Austin Lodge Road,
Eynsford, Kent. Tel: 0689 45778.
LANCASHIRE
Bobbin Mills SG, Bobbin Mill,
Scorton, Lancs. Tel: 0524 791507.
Deerplay CPC, Deerplay Inn,
Burnley Road, Bacup, Lancs. Tel:
0706 875917.
Fluke Hall SG, Fluke Hall, Pilling,
Preston, off A588, Lancs. Tel:
039130 745.
Hesketh GC, Guide Road, Hesketh
Bank, near Preston, Lancs. Tel:
077473 4114.
Kelbrook SS, The Shooting Lodge,
Kellbrook Moor, Foulridge, Colne,
Lancs. Tel: 0254 663547 (day) 0282
861632 (evenings).
Lancashire GC, The Bowers
Restaurant, Longmoor Lane,

Nateby, Garstang, Lancs. Tel: 09952
4251/2120.
North-East Lancashire GC,
Foxendole Lane, Higham, Lancs.
Tel: 0282 692440.
Overton & DGC, Heysham Industrial
Estate, Middleton Road, Middleton,
near Morecombe, Lancs. Tel: 0524
732875.
Rochdale GC, Fairview Inn, Broad
Lane, Rochdale, Lancs. Tel: 0706
31047.
Shaw & Compton CPC, Pingot SG,
Buckstones Road, Shaw, Oldham,
Lancs. Tel: 061-688 0187.
Sportsman's Arms GC, Kebcote,
Todmorden, Lancs. Tel: 0422
843274.
Westhoughton GC, Reeves House
Farm, Westhoughton, near Bolton,
Lancs. Tel: 0942 812022.
LEICESTERSHIRE
Bagworth Miners CPC, Bagworth
Colliery, Station Road, Bagworth,
Leics. Tel: 0530 60824.
Donington Park SG, Donington
Racetrack, Castle Donington. Tel:
0332 810048.
Leicestershire WA, on A6 one mile
south of Kibworth, Leics. Tel: 0536
203626 (day)/053753 2007
(evenings).
Market Harborough & DSC, on A6,
1 mile north of Market Harborough,
Leics. Tel: 0858 62847.
Melton Mowbray & DGC, Wycombe
Road, Scalford, Melton Mowbray,
Leics. Tel: 066476 685/615.
Thurlaston GC, Normanton Park,
Thurlaston, Leics. Tel: 045524 210.
LINCOLNSHIRE
Crowland Gc, Crowland Wash,
A1073, Lincs. Tel: 0733 62971.
East Coast GC, Spinney SG,
Willoughby, Alford, Lincs. Tel: 0754
72528.
Glen Bank GC, Old Folkingham
Airfield, Aslackby. Tel: 0778 423047.
Manby GC, Spinney Sg, Willoughby,
Alford, Lincs. Tel: 0507 604686/
60335.
Sutton Bridge GC, Chalk Lane,
Sutton Bridge, Spalding, Lincs. Tel:
0406 350188.
Waddington GC, Somerton Gate
Lane, Waddington, Lincoln, Tel:
0522 720982.

MIDDLESEX
Holland & Holland SS, Ducks Hill
Road, Northwood, Middx. Tel: 09274
25349.
West London SG, West End Road,
Northolt, Middx. Tel: 01-845 1377.
NORFOLK
Mid-Norfolk SS, Deighton Hills,
Taverham, Norfolk. Tel: 0603
860436.
Old Hall GC, Old Hall Farm, Hall
Lane, North Tuddenham, Norfolk.
Tel: 0362 860205.
Wayland CG, Mount Pleasant Farm,
Carbrooke Lane, Shipdham, near
Thetford. Tel: 0362 820943.
NORTHANTS
Northampton GC, Sywell Range,
Kettering Road (A43), Northampton.
Tel: 078887 650.
NORTHUMBERLAND
Bywell SG, Bywell Farm, Felton,
Northumberland. Tel: 0661 25885.
NOTTINGHAM
Cavendish GC, Clipstone Drive,
Forest Town, Mansfield. Tel: 0623
25988.
Nottingham & DGC, on A614 near
junction with A6097. Tel: 0602
273492.
Stile Hollow SG, off A616 Ollerton-
Budby Road, Notts. Tel: 0602
632348.
OXFORDSHIRE
Brize Norton GC, Worsham Quarry,
Worsham, near Minster Lovell, Oxon.
Tel: 0993 3789.
Chilton GC, Prospect Farm, Chilton,
Oxon. Tel: 0734 594224 (day)/0734
341752 (evening).
Chilton/Payne Shooting, Sotwell
Hill Fruit Farm, High Road,
Brightwell-cum-Sotwell, near
Wallingford, Oxon. Tel: 0491 36450/
06286 61841.
Christmas Common CC,
Watlington Hill Farm, Watlington,
Oxon. Tel: 049 161 3385.
Marcham SG, Buildings Farm,
Gozzards Ford, Abingdon, Oxon. Tel:
0865 739644.
Oxford SG, Southcombe House,
Southern Bypass, South Hinksey,
Oxford. Tel: 0865 730940.
Plough SG, Radclive-Tucker
Nurseries, Folly Hill, Faringdon,
Oxon. Tel: 0295 65819.

Waterperry GC, Manor Farm, Waterperry, Oxon. Tel: 08447 263.

SHROPSHIRE
Bicton GC, Clun, Craven Arms, Salop. Tel: 05884 241.
Bridgnorth & DGC, Naboths Vineyard, Shipley Common, Pattingham, nr Wolverhampton. Tel: 0562 883092.
G.R. Bourne SG, College Fields Farm, Woore, Salop. Tel: 0782 625385 (day)/063081 317 (evening).
Swancote CC, Swancote, on A454, Wolverhampton Road, Bridgnorth, Shropshire. Tel: 07464 683.
West Midlands SG, Hodnet, Market Drayton, Shropshire. Tel: 093924 644.

SOMERSET
Ash SG, Stone Farm, Ash, Martock, Somerset. Tel: 0935 823319.
Cheddar Valley GC, Draycott Moor, Cheddar, Somerset. Tel: 0934 742563/743167.
Chilworthy GC, Sticklepath Farm, Combe-St-Nicholas, near Chard, Somerset. Tel: 4605 5612.
Popes CPC, Popes Field, High Ham, near Langport, Somerset. Tel: 0935 822139/04608 294.
Street & DGC, Ivyphone Farm, near Street, Somerset. Tel: 0458 475058/42334.

STAFFORDSHIRE
Bridge Edge SG, Broad Lane, Brown Edge, Stoke-on-Trent, Staffs. Tel: 0782 534750.
Garland's SG, Raddle Farm, Erdingale, Tamworth, Staffs. Tel: 082785 216.
Klondyke SG, Stanhope Arms Hotel, 2 miles from Burton-on-Trent, on A50, Staffs. Tel: 0283 214121.
Leek & DGC, Westwood Hall Farm, Leek, Staffs. Tel: 0538 386127.
Midlands Counties SG, Oakedge, Wolseley Bridge, near Rugeley. Tel: 021 236 7451/0785 44191.
North Staffs SG, Stoniford Lane, Aston Pipegate, Market Drayton, Salop. Tel: 063081 7069.
Oaklea SG, Whinney Hill, Stockton-on-Tees, Staffs. Tel: 0642 607060.
Offley Grove CPSC, Offley Grove Farm, Adbaston, Staffs. Tel: 0889 270497.
Ranton GC, Cotton Road, Ranton,

Stafford. Tel: 0785 43360/3621.
Rowley GC, Rowley House Farm, Croxton, Eccleshall, Staffs. Tel: 063082 248.
Yarlet GC, New Farm, Marston Lane, Yarlet, nr. Stafford, off A34. Tel: 0785 54466.
Yoxall & DGC, Kingstanding Airfield, Needwood, on B5234, Burton on Trent, Staffs. Tel: 0283 41251.

SUFFOLK
Badwell Ash CPC, Back Lane, Badwell Ash, Bury St Edmunds, Suffolk. Tel: 03598 547.
East Suffolk GC, Home Farm, Kettleburgh, Woodbridge, Suffolk. Tel: 072882 228.
High Lodge SS, Henham Park, Blythburgh, Suffolk. Tel: 0502 70709/0502 65125.
Hockwold Gc, Sunnyside, Weeting, Brandon, Suffolk. Tel: 0842 81162.
ICI GC, Drinkstone, near windmill, off A45 between Stowmarket and Bury St Edmunds, near Woolpit, Suffolk. Tel: 0449 612047/613161 ext 3328.
Lakenheath R & GC, RAF Station, Lakenheath, Brandon, Suffolk. Tel: 0223 844001.
Newmarket GC, Rectory Pits, Kennett, Newmarket, Suffolk. Tel: 0440 820394.
RAF Benwaters/Woodbridge R & GC, RAF Station Benwaters, Woodbridge, Suffolk. Tel: 03943 3737 ext 2371/0394 420225.

SURREY
Bisley GC, Bisley Camp, Brookwood, Woking, Surrey. Tel: 07372 42332.
Copthorne GC, Bakers Wood, between Newchapel & Effingham Park, on B2028, Surrey. Tel: 0293 583208.
North Downs SG, Hangingwood, Grangers Hill, Woldingham, Surrey.

SUSSEX
Catsfield Sc, Catsfield Place, Battle, Sussex. Tel: 04243 511.
Chalk Pits CPC, Alfriston, Sussex. Tel: 0323 899873.
East Sussex GC, Croughton Manor, Westfield, on Hastings-Ashford Road, Sussex. Tel: 0323 30678.
Lower Lodge SG, The Haven, near Billinghurst, off A29. Tel: 040381

4666.
Pease Pottage SG, New Pond, Pease Pottage, Crawley, Sussex. Tel: 0293 21664
Red Lion GC, Outback Farm, Nutley, signposted off A22. Tel: 0825 74646.
Royal Oak CPC, Wayfield Farm, Pyecombe, off A23, Sussex. Tel: 044482 461.
Woodcock Sporting Ltd, Swiffe Farm, Broad Oak, Heathfield, East Sussex. Tel: 04352 3684.

WARWICKSHIRE
Edge Hill SG, Nadbury House, Camp Lane on B4086, Ratley Warks, Tel: 0926 32216.
Norton Lindsey SS, Gannaway Wood, on B4095, 2 miles east of Claverdon. Tel: 0203 614356.
Upper Spring Farm SC, Gaydon, Warwicks. Tel: 0203 614356 or 0926 642242 (eves).

WEST MIDLANDS
Coventry SS & CPC, The Bund, Stoneleigh, opposite Abbey entrance on B4115. Tel: 0926 50829.
Wolverhampton CTC, Mill Hayes, Lawn Lane, Coven Heath, Wolverhampton. Tel: 0902 790992.

WILTSHIRE
Urchfont CPC, Redhorn Hill, Near Devizes, Wiltshire. Tel: 038084 233.
White Horse CPC, Old Yatesbury Camp, Yatesbury, off A4, near Calne, Wilts. Tel: 0793 23075.

WORCESTERSHIRE
Broomhall SG, Boreley, Ombersley, near Worcester. Tel: 0905 56286.

YORKSHIRE
Allerton Bywater Colliery CPC, opposite colliery, Allerton Bywater, Yorks. Tel: 0532 861342.
Batley & DGC, Birkby Brow Wood, Howden Clough, Birstal, near Leeds. Tel: 0924 407803.
East Yorkshire GC, Bycot SG, Cherry Burton, Beverley, East Yorkshire. Tel: 06964 276.
Eldwick GC, Heights Lane, Bingley, Leeds. Tel: 0532 507518.
Ganton SG, Wold Farm, Ganton, near Scarborough, North Yorkshire. Tel: 0757 704660.
Holmfirth SS, Edge End Farm, near Ford Inn on A635, Holmfirth, Huddersfield. Tel: 0484 682767.

Knaresborough & DGC, Hazel Bank, Knaresborough, North Yorkshire. Tel: 0423 66972.
Kostrop GC, Burnell Range, Knostrop Way, Leeds 9. Tel: 0532 650554.
North Wolds GC, Uncleby Wold, Kirby Underdale, N. Yorks. Tel: 07596 314.
North Yorkshire SG, Felixkirk, near Thirsk, North Yorkshire. Tel: 09012 2001.
Peak GC, Side of Totley Range, Bastow Road, Sheffield, Tel: 0742 680903.
Snydale GC, Cross Keys, Old Snydale, Pontefract, West Yorkshire. Tel: 0977 702678.
Welbury Grange GC, Welbury, Northallerton, North Yorkshire. Tel: 0609 774922.
Wensleydale GC, Victoria Arms, Worton on A684, Aysgarth (DTL)/ Angill Askrigg, East Moore Road off Leyburn to Hawes Road (Sporting). Tel: 09693 289.

WALES
Afan Valley FSS, Hafod Farm, Goytre, Port Talbot, West Glamorgan. Tel: 0639 894240/ 898429.
Caerwys GC, near Mold, Clwyd, North Wales. Tel: 0352 720476.
Count SG, Haverfordwest, Dyfed. Tel: 0437 3740.
Cryant GC, Cryant Common, near Neath, West Glamorgan. Tel: 0792 815136.
Cwmbran GC, Mountain Air Inn, Peny-r-Heal, Pontypool, Gwent, Tel: 06333 65182/2703.
Feinion SGC, Glyn Farm, near Llandinam, Llandidloes, Powys. Tel: 0686 27844 (day)/05512 2033 (evenings).
Frampton SG, Landow, near Bridgend, South Glamorgan. Tel: 0222 865947.
Llandegla CTC, Llandegla, Clwyd, North Wales, Tel: 0978 364158.
Monmouth GC, Halfway, Tal-y-coed, on B4233, Gwent. Tel: 0600 2150 (eve)/6444 (day).
Nelson SG, Cifynydd, near Pontypridd, Mid-Glamorgan. Tel: 0222 865947.
Severn WA, Salisbury Farm, St Brides Road, Magor, Newport,

Gwent. Tel: 0291 421737.
South Wales SC, Mynddislwyn
Mountain, Pontllanfraith, Gwent. Tel:
0495 221737.
Uskmouth CPSC, Uskmouth Power
Station, Newport, Gwent. Tel: 0633
421749/271186.

CHANNEL ISLANDS
Crabbe CPC, St Mary, Jersey. Tel:
0534 54022/76588.
Guernsey CPSC. Tel: 0481 25633/
38068.
Jersey CPC, Lecq Farm, St Ouen,

SCOTLAND
Aberdeen & DCPC. Tel: 03308 265
Balfron GC. Tel: 041 956 3814.
Bonnybridge GC. Tel: 0324
825782.
Brucklay GC. Tel: 0358 21829.
Caithness CPC. Tel: 0847 64860.
Cumbernauld & DGC. Tel: 02367
21848.
Dumfermline & DGC. Tel: 0383
721323/729546.
Dunoon & DGC. Tel: 036983 628.
East Fife CPC. Tel: 0334 72814.
Edzell GC. Tel: 03562 43420.

Egnamoss GC. Tel: 0307 64181.
Falkirk & DGC. Tel: 0506 845129.
Fort William GC. Tel: 0397 4694.
Hardy's SG. Tel: 0307 66635.
Highland Deephaven CPC. Tel:
0349 830115.
Inverurie GC. Tel: 0467 20310.
Keith & Elgin GC. Tel: 0343 3856.
Kippen GC. Tel: 0259 216899.
Knapdale GC. Tel: 05467 651
Loch Ness GC. Tel: 04564 253.
Lorn GC. Tel: 0631 64672.
Loundoun GC. Tel: 0563 38768.
Lower Deeside Gc. Tel: 0224
733402.
Nairn GC. Tel: 0667 54507.
North Ayrshire. Tel: 029483 2231.
Peat Inn SG. Tel: 0382 541228.
Rowallan GC. Tel: 0563 38768.
Roy Bridge GC, Tel: 0397 4160.
Sea Side GC. Tel: 0224 733728
(day)/878646.
Strathoykel, Rosenhall & Lairg
GC. Tel: 0549 2025.
Taynuilt GC. Tel: 08662 648
Thornhill GC. Tel: 0848 30507.
West of Scotland SG. Tel: 041 956
1733.

SHOTGUN GLOSSARY

The following is a list of technical or semi-technical terms that may be useful to any newcomers to the shooting scene.

Action The body of the gun which contains the main moving parts. It may be either a boxlock or a side-lock. The latter has more moving parts and is usually more expensive to produce; it is similar to a hammer gun but with the hammers inside rather than outside the side plates. Some boxlock guns are fitted with side plates, which can make them resemble side-locks.

Anson & Deeley The designers of a standard boxlock action on which may modern actions are based.

Barrels The tubes through which the pellets are discharged.

Barrel selector A catch or button on a gun with a single selective trigger which enables the shooter to choose which barrel will fire first.

Bent The notch in the tumbler, into which the sear fits when the gun is cocked.

Bifurcated This basically means 'dividing into two'. When used to describe a gun's jointing, its significance is that it sometimes enables a shallower action to be made.

Bite The notch in the lump into which a locking bolt fits.

Blacking Normally a chemically produced, rust resistant finish.

Bore The inside of a barrel; (**see gauge**).

Boxlock A type of action, in which the locks are not mounted on side plates, but within the action frame.

Breech The end of the barrel into which the cartridges are inserted.

Butt The part of the stock that seets into the shooter's shoulder.

Cartridge cap The percussion cap situated in the centre of the cartridge head. When struck by the firing pin or striker this ignites the powder and fires the cartridges.

Case hardening A process by which the surface of the action is treated to reduce wear.

Cast The degree to which the stock deviates horizontally from a straight line extended back from the centre line of the barrels.

Chamber The section of the barrel at the breech end of which the cartridge is inserted.

Chequering	Patterns cut in the wood at the parts which are touched by the shooter's hands, to give a surer grip.
Choke	A constriction at the muzzle end of a barrel, intended to vary the size and density of the pattern. It varies roughly from five to 40 thous. (thousandths of an inch). Improved cylinder is approximately five thous., or points of choke, quarter choke is 10 thous., half choke is 20 thous., three-quarter choke is 30 thous., and full choke is 40 thous.
Chopper lump	One of the methods of joining the barrels to the action. Each barrel is forged with the lump integral to it at the breech end, and the lumps are then joined together, usually by brazing.
Chrome plating	A practice that is popular on the continent. Applied to the bore, it is intended to resist corrosion.
Comb	The top of the stock, behind the hand. A monte Carlo stock has a comb which runs parallel with the line of the barrels, and is then generally 'notched' down to the heel.
Cross pin	As **Hinge Pin**.
Drop	The distance which the comb and heel are below a straight line extended back from the top of the rib.
Ejectors	Shaped pieces of metal powered by springs which fire the empty cartridge cases out of the breech. On double guns they are usually selective – ejecting only cartridges that have been fired.
Engraving	A pattern cut into the metal, normally on the action body, for aesthetic purposes.
Extractor	This pushes the empty case clear of the breech so that it can be removed.
Firing pin	As **Striker**.
Floating	Applied to barrels. It means that they are not fixed rigidly at the muzzle end and can therefore expand independently without distortion.
Fore-end	The wooden part under the barrels wich contains the fore-end iron and sometimes the ejector springs and/or kickers.
Full gape	Describes the distance to which the barrels open away from the action.
Gauge	Describes the size or calibre of a barrel. A 12 gauge (or bore) barrel has a tube diameter roughly the size of a round lead ball, 12 of which would weigh 1 lb. The same principle applies for 8 bore, 20 bore, etc. This does not hold for the .410, however, which denotes the approximate measurement of the barrel diameter.
Hammer	The part of the gun which hits the striker. On most modern guns it is sited inside the action and is called a tumbler.
Hammerless	Where the hammers have been moved inside the action. They are now generally known as tumblers.
Heel	The point at the top rear of the stock.

Hinge pin	The pin on which a gun hinges when it is opened.
Jointing	The method of joining the barrels to the action.
Lock	The moving parts of the action – sears, springs, tumblers, etc.
Lump	A protrusion at the end of the barrels, used in conjunction with the locking bolt or bolts to hold the barrels and action together.
Magazine	The part in which extra cartridges are held on semi-automatic and pump action guns. Such guns often have a capacity of one cartridge in the chamber and four in the magazine.
Monobloc	As **Sleeving**.
Overdraft	When the barrels do not stay at full gape as intended. It can have a number of causes and makes reloading more difficult, particularly the bottom barrel of O/U.
Patterns	This describes the way the pellets in a shot charge are distributed when fired from a gun. Modern guns and cartridges tend to throw 'tight' patterns. The only sure way to check and test patterns is to shoot the gun at a pattern plate from an accurately measured distance, and then count the pellets. At least six shoots should be fired from each barrel.
Proof	All guns must be passed for proof before being sold in this country. This may be carried out at the London or Birmingham Proof Houses, or at an accepted foreign proof house. Theoretically, a gun that has passed proof should be safe to use with cartridges and at the pressures specified.
Pump action:	Single barrel repeating gun. When a cartridge is fired to the shooter 'trombones' the fore-end back and forwards. This ejects the fired case and reloads the empty chamber with an unfired cartridge from the magazine.
Recoil	The 'blow' which the gun gives the shooter when it is fired – following the old physics principle that there is no action without reaction. W.W. Greener had a formula that gun weight should be 96 time that of the shot charge if excessive recoil was to be avoided – this means a 1 oz. load in a 6 lb. gun, for example. Given a gun with correct headspace and chamber length, this still holds good today. With heavily built people and women, the shape of the butt is particularly critical in ensuring that the recoil is evenly spread.
Recoil pad	A ventilated rubber extension to the stock, which can soften the blow of recoil.
Ribs	Strips of metal, normally above and below the barrels on a side-by-side. There may be three on an over-and-under – one at each side between the barrels and one on top. The top rib is an aid to pointing the gun and may be of various widths and designs.
Safety and safety catches	The majority of guns have safeties that block the movement of the triggers. They do not prevent the sear being jarred

	out of the bent. Catches may be automatic – in that they are set to 'safe' every time the top lever is pressed or the gun opened – or manual.
Sear	The small arm which holds the tumbler at full cock, and is released when the trigger is pulled.
Semi-automatic	Single barrel, repeating gun. Usually gas or recoil operated.
Shot string	The extent to which the shot spreads lengthways. The length of shot string can be influenced by many things, including the hardness of the pellets, the type of wad or wadding, the type of choke and the shape of the pellets. Badly formed pellets of varying shapes will usually produce longer shot strings.
Sidelock	A type of action, closely related to hammer guns. Generally more expensive than a boxlock, the locks are mounted on side plates. Often thought to give better trigger pulls.
Sights	Usually plastic or metal beads at the muzzle end of the top rib, and sometimes in the centre.
Sleeving	The process in which the lumps are machined from a solid block forging or casting. The block is bored to take the barrels, which are usually soldered in. This method is excellent for modern production techniques and makes for a strong joint. This system is also well suited to repair work.
Spread	The diameter of the shot pattern. Wider spreads are required for some forms of shooting tnan for others.
Stock	The wooden part at the rear of the gun. This may have a straight hand, semi-pistol or full pistol grip.
Striker	Also known as the firing pin. The part which actually hits the cartridge cap. On modern guns it is normally separate from the tumbler.
Thous	Thousandths of an inch.
Toe	The point at the bottom rear of the stock.
Top extension	Extension of tops of barrels at breech end.
Top lever	The lever on top of the action which is pushed in order to open the gun.
Trigger	The part which the shooter pulls to fire the gun. There may be two on a double barrelled gun, in which case the front trigger usually fires the right barrel on a side-by-side and the bottom barrel on an over-and-under. Single triggers may be selective or non-selective.
Trigger plate	The plate to which the trigger assembly is fitted. A trigger plate action is one in which most of the striker mechanism is fixed to the trigger plate and can be removed as a unit.
Trigger pulls	The weight and length of the movement required to fire the gun.
Tubes	Barrels.
Tumbler	The part inside the action which is released when the

shooter pulls the trigger. it is powered by a main spring and
hits the striker into the cartridge cap.

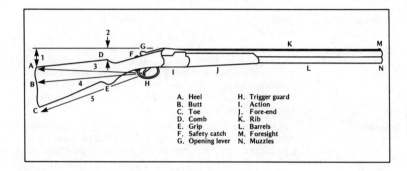

A.	Heel	H.	Trigger guard
B.	Butt	I.	Action
C.	Toe	J.	Fore-end
D.	Comb	K.	Rib
E.	Grip	L.	Barrels
F.	Safety catch	M.	Foresight
G.	Opening lever	N.	Muzzles

GUNSHOPS

The following list of gunshops does not purport to be a comprehensive list of all the retail trade outlets. The shops have been selected to provide suitable lists of outlets in each area. Some of the shops listed are GTA members where customers may be assured of receiving good service.

AVON

Avon Shooting Ltd
2 Market Place, Radstock, Avon, BA3 3AE.
Tel: 0761 33167

G J Bissex (Avon Shooting) Ltd
Hollowdene, 2 Market Place, Radstock.
Tel: 0761 33167

County Firearms
'Woodlands' Warminster Road, Nr Claverton, Bath.
Tel: 022122 2224

I M Crudgington Ltd
37 Broad Street, Bath, BA1 5LT.
Tel: 0225 64928/66325

Dan-Arms (UK) Ltd
Unit 7, Hortonwood 33, Telford, Shropshire, TF1 4EX.
Tel: 0952 608047

Fish 'n' Shoot
5 Cleveland Place East, Bath.
Tel: 0225 336620

George Gibbs Ltd
3-4 Perry Road, Park Row, Bristol, BS1 5BQ.
Tel: 0272 248 24
Gunmakers, retailers and repairs. We are also game fishing specialists. Open 6 days a week 9.15 am to 5.00 pm.

J B Sports
3 Repton Road, Sandy Park, Brislington, Bristol.
Tel: 0272 772633

Rowland's Limited
15 Green Street, Bath, BA1 2JZ.
Tel: 0225 62911

Scott Tackle (R Crocker & P Kent)
42 Soundwell Road, Staple Hill, Bristol, BS16 4QP.

Sheppard's Rod, Gun & Sports Centre
46 Bond Street, Bristol, BS1 3LZ.
Tel: 0272 273351

BEDFORDSHIRE

Airmasters
2 Hibbert Street, Luton, Beds, LU1 3UU.
Tel: 0582 26217
Specialists in superior customised airweapons. Manufacturers of targets and general accessories. Stockist of leading makes of air weapons, scopes, clothing, pellets and all general shooting accessories. Open 9.30-6.00 Mon-Sat.

Bedford Target Supplies
Duck Mill Lane, Bedford.
Tel: 0234 217838/9
The Shooting Specialist. A large selection of equipment for both the beginner and the experienced shooter. Shotguns, sporting air rifles and pistols. Complete range of accessories. Comprehensive gunsmithing service. Open Monday to Saturday 9-6.

Bleak Hall Bird Farm (Kempston) Ltd
1 High Street, Kempston, Bedford

W Darlow
46 Ashburnham Road, Bedford, MK40 1EE
Tel: 0234 52056

Duglan & Cooper Ltd
14–16 Church Street, Dunstable.
Tel: 0582 64649

John Eastaff
Elstow Storage Depot, Kempston
Hardwick, Bedford.
Tel: 0234 740834

Tom Lindars
82 North Street, Leighton Buzzard.
Tel: 0525 372416

BERKSHIRE
Astral Sports
86 Northbrook Street, Newbury.
Tel: 0635 35166

K C Sports
24-26 Barkham Road, Wokingham,
Berkshire.
Tel: 0734 781712

Roxton Sporting Ltd
10 Bridge Street, Hungerford.
Tel: 0488 82885

Slough Sports & Angling Centre
245 Farnham Road, Slough,
Berkshire.
Tel: 0753 21055

Thomas Turner Gunmaker
208 Gosbrook Road, Caversham,
Reading, RG4 88L.
Tel: 0734 481699

Windsor Guns & Field Sports
9 St Leonards Road, Windsor.
Tel: 0753 854023

BUCKINGHAMSHIRE
Jason Abbot Gunmakers Ltd
1-3 Bell Street, Princes Risborough,
HP17 0AD.
Tel: 08444 6677/6672

Benskins County Sports
15 Market Square, Winslow.
Tel: 029671 2580

Berdan (Gunmakers) Ltd
Unit 1, Rabans Close, Rabans Lane
Ind. Est., Aylesbury, HP10 3RT.
Tel: 0296 87408

Cox The Saddler
23 High Street, Chesham, HP5 1BG.
Tel: 0494 771340

Fish & Field
62 Nelson Street, Buckingham.
Tel: Buckingham 814495

**Hartmann & Weiss Ltd
(Gunmaker)**
Folly Meadow, Hammersley Lane,
Penn.
Tel: 049481 2836

Rods 'n' Guns
Rickmansworth Lane, Chalfont
St Peter, SL9 0JR.
Tel: 024 027 5326

Wooburn Green Guns
6 The Green, Wooburn Green.
Tel: 062 85 28718

Wycombe Armoury Ltd
Westbourne Street, High Wycombe,
HP11 2PZ.
Tel: 0494 30677

CAMBRIDGESHIRE
John Bradshaw
Perio Mill, Fortheringhay,
Peterborough, PE8 5HU.
Tel: 08326 376 (24 hours)
*Guns, ammunition, shooting &
sporting accessories. Part exchanges
welcome. We stock a large range of
sporting rifles including air rifles &
shotguns. Most makes & models
available.*

The Cambridgeshire Gun Centre
243-245 Newmarket Road,
Cambridge.
Tel: 0223 322161

J A Cochrane & Son
24-25 Old Market, Wisbech,
PE13 1NB

Gallyons
5 Cowgate, Peterborough.
Tel: 0733 43152

Sheltons Gun and Tackle
67 South Street, Stanground,
Peterborough.
Tel: 0733 65287

Theoben Engineering
Stephenson Road, St Ives,
Huntingdon, Cambs, PE17 4WJ
Tel: 0480 61718

Thornton & Son
46-47 Burleigh Street, Cambridge,
CB1 1DJ.
Tel: 0223 358709

P G Woodward
Daintree Road, Ramsey St Mary,
Huntingdon, PE17 1T.
Tel: 073129 354

**A W Wright & Sons, Fenland
Gunsmith Ltd**
98 Creek Road, March, PE15 8RO.
Tel: 0354 53290

CHANNEL ISLANDS

M F Gotel Guns
14 Brighton Road, St Helier, Jersey.
Tel: 0534 76588

The Gun Shop
7 Hauterville, St Peter Port, Guernsey
Tel: 0481 22409

Newton & Newton Ltd
3 Colomberie Parade, St Helier,
Jersey.
Tel: 0534 33697

CHESHIRE

A Branthwaite
6-8 Ravenoak Road, Cheadle Hulme,
Cheshire.
Tel: 061 485 1199

Chester Gun Company (M & A Foxton)
23 Charles Street, Hoole, Chester.
Tel: 0244 314694

The Countryman
Holly Bank, Manchester Road,
Rixton, Warrington.
Tel: 061 775 2842

Henry Monk (Gunmaker) Ltd
8 Queen Street, Chester, CH1 3LG.
Tel: 0244 29088
Game, guns, rifles, clothing, knives, game fishing tackle. A huge selection of books on shooting, fishing, dogs and their training and so much more.

H G Hopkins & Sons (Gunmakers)
53-55 High Street, Sandbach.
Tel: 09367 2404

E Jackson Gunsmith
37 Chester Road, Whitby, South
Wirral.

Kab's Cabin
228 Broad Street, Crewe, Cheshire.
Tel: 0270 212708

Keep Nets & Cages
4 Queens Parade, Winsford.
Tel: 060 65 54363

Lymm Sports Centre
8 The Cross, Lymm, Cheshire.
Tel: 092 575 3021
Specialists in all target disciplines. Gun repair. Firearms, shotguns & air weapons supplied & repaired.

North Wales Shooting School
Sealand Manor, Sealand, Chester.
Tel: 0244 812219

Pennine Leisure
Brookside Mill, Union Street/Crossall
Street, Macclesfield, Cheshire.
Tel: 0625 20167

T T Proctor Ltd
88a Water Lane, Wilmslow.
Tel: 0625 526654

Sporting & Militaria Arms Ltd
Kerfield House, Knutsford.
Tel: 0565 3344/4861

CLEVELAND

Bob Dunkley's Firearms
Unit 4, The Arcade, Redcar,
Cleveland.
Tel: 0642 486000

John F Gent Ltd
Firearms & Fishing Tackle Ltd,
161 York Road, Hartlepool, TS26 9EQ.
Tel: 0429 72585

J W Simpson
6 Bridge Road, Stokesley.
Tel: 0642 711892

A. Ward Thompson
5-6 Albert Road, Stockton-onTees.
Tel: 0642 607060

CORNWALL

Bay Tree Arms
10 Baytree Hill, Liskeard.
Tel: Liskeard 46636
For rifles, shot guns and pistols. All accessories – also repairs.

Country Sports
Crantock Street, Newquay.

Roy Dutch Firearms
2 East Hill, St Austell.
Tel: 0726 72960

Forsyth Firearms
St Mary's Street, Truro.
Tel: 0872 71744

A B Harvey & Son Ltd
1-2 Market Strand, Falmouth, TR11
3DA.
Tel: 0326 312796

Helston Gunsmiths
The Clies, Meneage St, Helston.
Tel: 03265 3385. Telex: 45117 G.

Tony Kennedy Guns
6 Church Street, Launceston.
Tel: 0566 4465

John Langdon

20 St Mary Street, Truro, TR1 2AF.

Lower Lake Shooting Grounds
Upton Cross, Liskeard.
Tel: 0579 62319

Southern Gun Co
4 Market Street, Bodmin.
Tel: 0208 5915

Tackle Box
4 Market Square, Mevagissey.
Tel: 072684 3513

R Drew Whurr (Specialist Gunsmith)
The Old Mill House, Helland Bridge, Bodmin, PL30 4QR.
Tel: St Mabyn (020884) 206

CUMBRIA

Thomas Atkinson & Son
14 Stricklandgate, Kendal, Cumbria.
Tel: 0539 20300

Border Guns
10 Botchergate, Carlisle, Cumbria.
Tel: 0228 49159

Cumbria Countryman
Market Place, Ambleside.
Tel: 096 63 3145

N John Ferguson
43 Fisher Street, Workington.
Tel: 0900 61559

Grahams Guns & Tackle
17 Fisher Street, Workington, Cumbria.
Tel: 0900 5093

Gun Shop, Ian Nicholson
Jubilee Bridge, Cockermouth.
Tel: 0900 822058

Hannays Fishing Tackle and Guns
50-52 Crellin Street, Barrow in Furness, Cumbria.
Tel: 0229 22571

W N Holmes & Son
45 Main Street, Egremont.
Tel: 820368

Mr J W McHardy
South Henry Street, Carlisle, Cumbria.
Tel: 0228 23988

John Norris of Penrith
21/22 Victoria Road, Penrith.
Tel: 0768 64211

R Raine & Co
21 Warwick Road, Carlisle, Cumbria.
Tel: 0228 23009

R A Sanders (Firearms)
Rocklands, Hard Cragg, Cartmel, Grange Over Sands, Cumbria.
Tel: 044854 476

Charles R Sykes
4 Great Dockray, Penrith.
Tel: 0768 62418

Wells (Barrow) Ltd
56 Crellin Street, Barrow-in-Furness.
Tel: 0229 22681

Geoff Wilson Practical Gunsmiths
36 Portland Place, Carlisle, Cumbria CA1 1RL.
Tel: 0228 31542

DERBYSHIRE

K Bancroft
82 Spire Hollin, Glossop, Derbys.
Tel: 04574 2599
All types of new and second hand shotguns including Winchester/ Parker Hale. Also rifles and pistols, ammo etc. Resident working gunsmith.

J V Burrows Guns & Antiques
Sheeplea, Baslow Road, Eastmoor, Chesterfield.

Derby Shooting Supplies Ltd
1 and 3 Peel Street, Derby.
Tel: 0332 369500

Fosters Sporting Services Ltd
32 St John Street, Ashbourne.
Tel: 0335 43135

F Hall Gunmakers Ltd
Beetwell Street, Chesterfield, S40 1SH.
Tel: 0246 73133

Hilton Gun Co
62 Station Road, Hatton.
Tel: 0283 814141/814463

Matlock Gun Co
61/63 Smedley Street, East Matlock.
Tel: 0629 3892

J F Neville
6 King Street, Alfreton.
Tel: 0773 834451
All leading makes of shotguns at competitive prices. Part/ex welcome. Repairs and alterations by own gunsmith. Guns and ammunition and clothing. Open 9.30-5.30 Mon-Sat, Thurs 7pm. Closed all day Wednesday.

W Parr (Firearms) International
32 Market Place, Belper, EE5 1F2.

Tel: 0773 826955
Largest gunshop in the Midlands. Over 500 guns in stock, including sporting and military rifles. Extensive shooting accessories dept. Closed Wednesday, late night Friday 9.00am-8.00pm.

Yeaveley Shooting Ground
New Close Farm, Yeaveley, Ashbourne, Derbys, DE6 2DT.
Tel: 033 523 247

DEVON

Atwell & Phipps, The Gunsmiths
16 Litchdon Street, Barnstaple.
Tel: 0271 7807

L J Brookes & Son 'Gunsmiths'
The Torbay Gun Shop, 36 South Street, Torquay.
Tel: 0803 211364
Repairs, overhauls, tuition. Registered firearms dealer Devon and Cornwall 299.

Country Sports
9 William Street, Tiverton.
Tel: 0884 254770

County Sports Ltd
105 Boutport Street, Barnstaple, Devon.
Tel: Barnstaple 46689
Stockists of all types, shotguns, pistols & air rifles. Clothing, ammunition, decoys, fishing and other sports.

Drum Sports Ltd
47 Courtnay Street, Newton Abbot, Devon.
Tel: 0626 65333
Pop in for our guns and accessories range which includes air rifles and pistols, cartridge belts and bags, rifle slings and an excellent selection of Barbour clothing.

E Gale & Son Ltd
2-3 Mill Street, Bideford.
Tel: 02372 72508

Gun & Sort Shop, The
76 Fore Street, Heavitree, Exeter, EX1 2RR.
Tel: 0392 71701
Specialist gun, pistol and rifle stockists. Air rifles ammunition, knives, fishing tackle and militaria weapons. We buy guns, rifles and accessories.

Gun Room, The
2 Church Street, Modbury, Ivybridge.
Tel: Modbury 830203

Gun Room & Sports Centre
139 High Street, Ilfracombe.
Tel: 0271 64546
Stockists of Browning, Miroku, Beretta etc. Large range of guns can be tried before purchase.

Keep, The
30 Brook Street, Tavistock.
Tel: 0822 2509

Ladd's Guns & Sports
86/87 High Street, Crediton, Devon.
Tel: 03632 2666
Good selection of specialist rifles, pistols and shotgun ammunition. All accessories Barbour clothing – all at competitive prices.

Mayson Firearms
170 Grenville Road, St Judes, Plymouth.
Tel: 0752 266436

Molyneux Sports of
26 Fore Street, Kingsbridge, Devon.
Tel: Kingsbridge 2176
Everything for the outdoor sportsman, comprehensive selection of shooting equipment, shotguns, ammunition, air weapons, knives, sheaths and carriers. Leading clothing agencies held with mail order service available.

M J W Sports Ltd
7/7a Dartmouth, Paignton.

Neroche Armoury
High Street, Honiton.
Tel: 0404 2100

'O L W' Sports
36 Fore Street, Buckfastleigh, Devon.
Tel: Buckfastleigh 43004
Shotguns, new and second hand. Small arms, ammunition, decoys. All shooting accessories. Vast collection of clothing plus country sports equipment.

Frank Richard (Gunsmiths)
25 Silver Street, Taunton.
Tel: 0823 81487

Sportsman, The
7 Dartmouth Road, Paignton, TQ5AB.
Tel: 0803 558142/551275

Staffords Gunsmiths

279 Union Street, Plymouth.
Tel: 0752 664865

Stanley's Tackle Centre
12 Middle Street, Brixham.
Tel: Brixham 3080

The Torbay Gun Shop
36 South Street, Torbay

John Webber (Sports)
79 Queen Street, Exeter.
Tel: 0392 74975

Wheelers Sports
44 Fore Street, Totnes, S Devon.
Tel: Totnes 865174
*For guns, pistols and all shooting
equipment, cartridges, clays, decoys
etc. Barbour clothing stocked. Ring us
for quotes on the above items.
Competitive prices guaranteed.*

DORSET

Arthur Conyers Ltd
3 West Street, Blandford.
Tel: 0258 52307

Edgcumbe Arms (Gunmakers) Ltd
1/11 Randolph Road, Parkstone,
Poole.
Tel: 0202 740743
Subsidiary of Majex (UK) Ltd.

Gunsports
871 Christchurch Road, Pokesdown,
Bournemouth.
Tel: 0202 425735

Gunstock
23 Church Road, Parkstone, Poole.
Tel: 02027 35296

Messrs Hayman
13 Trinity Road, Weymouth

C Jeffrey & Sons
25 High East Street, Dorchester.

John March (Firearms) Ltd
19 Westborough, Wimborne.
Tel: 0202 888504

Modern & Antique Firearms
147 Tuckton Road, Bournemouth.
Tel: 0202 429369

Sport Equip
37 High Street, Shaftsbury.
Tel: Shaftsbury 2511

Wessex Gun Sales
Clay Pigeon Cafe, Wardon Hill, Nr
Dorchester.
Tel: 093 58 3368

DURHAM

Messrs W P Adams
42 Duke Street, Darlington.
Tel: 0325 468 069
Also at 9 Princes Road,
Middlesbrough (Tel: 0642 210706)

**A & J Corbett Guns, Cartridges,
Clothing Etc**
Greenfoot, Stanhope.
Tel: 0388 528306

Elvet Game Centre
8 New Elvet, Durham City.
Tel: 0388 819500

Fosters Country Sport
1 Cleveland Street, Darlington.
Tel: 0325 51351

Matched Pairs Ltd
20 High St, Spennymoor, Co Durham.
Tel: 0388 819500

A Ward Thompson
5/6 Albert Road, Stockton On Tees,
Cleveland.

F E Wilkinson (Guns)
40 Horsemarket, Barnard Castle.
Tel: 0833 31118

ESSEX

All Seasons Leisure Centre
1 Old Mill Parade, Victoria Road,
Romford, Essex.
Tel: 0708 23740
*Replica guns, martial arts equipment,
survival aids, military clothing etc.*

Air Gun Centre
107 London Road, Rayleigh.
Tel: 0268 771730

Alexandra Guns Ltd
54 Alexandra Street, Southend on
Sea.
Tel: 0702 339349

Brentwood Gun Co
31 Hutton Road, Shenfield,
Brentwood.
Tel: 0277 212621

Budget Guns & Tackle
44/45 Duke Street, Chelmsford.
Tel: 0245 353715

Budget Guns & Tackle
13 Grange Way, Colchester.
Tel: 0206 65333

Ronnie Crowe
63 Maldon Road, Great Baddow,

Chelmsford.
Tel: 0245 71246

Messrs Emson & Son
86 High Street, Earls Colne,
Colchester.
Tel: 07875 3413

Essex Gun
6 Eastbrook Drive, Rush Green,
Romford.
Tel: 01 593 3502

Grange Gun Co
107 London Road, Rayleigh, Essex.
Tel: Rayleigh 771730
Beretta custom grade dealer, Victory cartridges and everything for the shooting man. Closed all day Wednesday.

Hides & Deec's
Pesterford Bridge, Stansted.
Tel: 0279 812638/813685

May of London (Gunmakers) Ltd
35 Cherry Tree Rise, Buckhurst Hill,
Essex.
Tel: 01 504 5946

Phoenix Gun Co
208 Leigh Road, Leigh on Sea.
Tel: 0702 714872

K D Radcliffe Ltd
150 High Street, Colchester.
Tel: 0206 572758

Roding Armoury (Gunsmiths)
Silver Street, Market Place, Abridge,
Romford, Essex.
Tel: 037 881 3570

W Schafle & Co
1 Military Road, Colchester.
Tel: 0206 572270

South East Essex Gun Club
Pickerels Farm, Watery Lane,
Battlebridge, Essex.
Tel: 0277 233468
Open fortnightly on Saturdays, 11am onwards. Tuition free to club members. Skeet and DTL practice with trophy competitions for club members.

J E Spalding
112 East Road, West Mersea.
Tel: 020638 2477

Russell Walkyier
17 High Street, Saffron Walden.
Tel: 0799 23430

A & D Wheeler 'Guns'
Wethersfield Road, Sible Hedingham,

Halstead.

GLOUCESTERSHIRE

Allsports
126/128 Eastgate Street, Gloucester.
Tel: 0452 27324/22756

Chambers & Co Gunmakers
Ideal Gunworks, Northleach.
Tel: 04516 372

F J Cole (Cirencester) Ltd
26 Castle Street, Cirencester.
Tel: 025 3832

Ian Coley
442/444 High Street, Cheltenham.
Tel: 0242 582270/522443

Corinium Gunsmiths
26 Castle Street, Cirencester, GL7
1QH.
Tel: 0285 67527

Forest of Dean Armoury
Canberra New Road, Coalway,
Coleford.
Tel: 0594 33908

Gloucester Rod & Gun Room
67 Alvin Street, Gloucester.
Tel: 0452 410444

Roxton Sporting Ltd
3/5 West Market Place, Cirencester.
Tel: 0285 69033

Shipston Gun Co Ltd
Blenheim Farm, Moreton in Marsh.
Tel: 0608 50349

GREATER LONDON

Bapty & Co Ltd
703 Harrow Road, London.
Tel: 01 969 6671

**Thomas Bland & Sons
(Gunmakers) Ltd**
21/22 New Row, St Martins Lane,
London.
Tel: 01 836 9122

Boss & Co Ltd
13 Dover Street, London.
Tel: 01 493 1127

British Sports
107 Praed Street, 15 Norfolk Place,
Paddington, W2 1NT.
Tel: 01 402 7511, 3 lines

Catford Gun Co
9 Eros House, Catford.
Tel: 01 697 0830

Chubbs of Edgware (Gunmakers) Ltd.
33 South Parade, Mollison Way, Edgware.
Tel: 01 952 1579

Cogswell & Harrison (Gun Agency)
5 King Street, Covent Garden, London, WC2E 8HN.
Tel: 01 240 3186

Collins Brothers (Southern Armoury) Ltd
171 New Kent Road, Nr Elephant & Castle.
Tel: 01 407 2278

D & P Guns
134 Blenheim Road, Harrow, Middlesex.
Tel: 01 863 5873

Empire Arms Co
14 Empire Parade, Great Cambridge Road, Edmonton, London, N18 1AA.
Tel: 01 807 3802

William Evans Ltd
67a St James Street, London
Tel: 01 493 0415

C Farlow & Co Ltd
5 Pall Mall, London.
Tel: 01 839 2423

Field Arms Ltd
10 Tilney Street, Audley Square, London.

Fulham Armoury Ltd
185 Fulham Palace Road, London, W8 8QX.
Tel: 01 385 9902

Guncraft
11 Woodcock Hill, Kenton, Harrow, HA3 OXP.
Tel: 01 907 3651

The Gun Makers Co
The Proof House, 48 Commercial Road, London.
Tel: 01 481 2695

Guns & Tackle
811 High Street, Whitton, Twickenham.
Tel: 01 898 3129

Harrisons Guns
10 Village Arcade, Station Road, Chingford, London, E4
Tel: 01 524 7491
Sporting, field, target shooting, air weapons, shotguns and shooting

accessories.

Hellis Beesley and Watson Gunmakers
33 South Parade, Mollison Way, Edgware.
Tel: 01 952 1579

Holland & Holland Ltd
33 Bruton Street, London.
Tel: 01 499 4411

Messrs Judds of Hillingdon
3 Westbourne Parade, Uxbridge Road, Hillingdon, Middlesex.
Tel: 01 573 0196

London Armoury
639 Commercial Road, London.
Tel: 01 790 6094.

London Gun Co
622 Greenford Road, Greenford, Middlesex.
Tel: 01 575 2934

Manor Firearms
421 High Street, Manor Park, London E12 6TL.
Tel: 01 552 9036

Parabellum Sports
475 Upper Richmond Road West, London.
Tel: 01 878 7003

Pax Guns Ltd
166 Archway Road, London.
Tel: 01 340 3039

James Purdey & Sons Ltd
Audley House, 57/58 South Audley Street, London.
Tel: 01 499 1801

John Rigby & Co (Gunmakers) Ltd
5 King Street, Covent Garden, London, WC2E 8HN.
Tel: 01 734 7611

J Roberts & Son
5 King Street, Covent Garden, London WC2E 8HN.
Tel: 01 240 3186
Gun Agency for Cogswell & Harrison

Shooters Supply Co Ltd
149 Cleveland Street, London
Tel: 01 387 8330

Solis Gunshop
487b Green Lanes, Haringey, London.
Tel: 01 340 9593

Stratford Gun Room

30 Vicarage Lane, London, E15.
Tel: 01 519 7411

Streatham Armoury
90 Mitcham Lane, London, SW16.
Tel: 01 769 0671

Thames Water Sports (Brian Fedder Investments) Ltd
179/181 Fulham Palace Road, London.
Tel: 01 381 0558

John Wilkes, The Gun & Rifle Makers
79 Beak Street, Regent Street, London, W1R 3LF.
Tel: 01 437 6539

Woodys of Wembley
565 High Road, Wembley.
Tel: 01 902 7217

GREATER MANCHESTER

Davies of Bolton
128 Deane Road, Bolton.
Tel: 0204 24893

John Dickson
128 Muldeth Road, Burnage, Manchester.
Tel: 061 445 2976

Hurley's Sports
93 Piccadilly, Manchester.
Tel: 061 228 2888

Manchester Air Guns
470 Oldham Road, Failsworth, Manchester.
Tel: 061 681 1671

Pearsons Tackle & Guns
292 Manchester Street, Oldham, Greater Manchester.
Tel: 061 633 6199

Penine Shooting Centre
Gorrels Way, Rochdale, OL11 2NR.
Tel: 0706 30502

T Stensby & Co Ltd
1 Shudehill, Manchester.
Tel: 061 834 6589

Weston Supplies
398/400 Ashton Road, Hathershaw, Oldham.

HAMPSHIRE

Astral Sports
18 New Market Square, Basingstoke.
Tel: 0256 22255

Bassetts
4-6 Swan Street, Petersfield.
Tel: 0730 64238

B E Chaplin (Gunmakers) Ltd
6 Southgate Street, Winchester.
Tel: 0962 52935

Cole & Son (Devizes) Ltd
67 High Street, Andover
Tel: 0264 51773

Custom Rifles
100f St Mary Street, Southampton.
Tel: 0703 30253
Stalking rifles, target rifles, bench rest rifles made to order.

Greenfield of Salisbury Ltd
16 Market Place, Ringwood.
Tel: 04254 3223

Gunmark Ltd
The Armoury, Fort Wallington, Fareham.
Tel: 0329 231531

Herriard Sporting Guns
Alton Road, Herriard, Basingstoke.
Tel: 025 683 277

Jennings & Paterson
High Street, Fareham.
Tel: 0329 234343

Lockerley Game Services
2 Barley Hill Cottages, Dumbridge, Romsey.
Tel: 0794 40851

Marlborough Gun Shop
138a Weyhill Road, Andover.
Tel: Andover 53957

Maskells Guns
18 Camp Road, Fanborough, Hampshire.
Tel: 0252 518062
Stockists for Webley, ASI, Weihrauch, BSF, Original Feinwerkan, Ensign and Sharp. Scopes by Tasco, Rhino, Kassmar, ASI. Large selection of pellets, gun covers and accessories.

McCrabtree
Portsmouth Gun Centre, 295 London Road, Portsmouth.

Modern & Antique Firearms
147 Tuckton Road, Southbourne, Bournemouth, BH6 3JZ.

Multi Sports (High Sarin Ltd)
225 Old Christchurch Road, Bournemouth.
Tel: 0202 26319

Parvin Brothers
79 High Street, West End,
Southampton.
Tel: 0703 465656

Portsmouth Gun Centre
295 London Road, Northend,
Portsmouth.
Tel: 0705 660574

Raison Brothers
2 Park Road, Farnborough,
Hampshire, GU14 6JG.

Southampton Firearms
100f St Mary Street, Southampton.
Tel: 0703 30253

Sporting & Firearms Centre
41 Brookley Road, Brockenhurst,
SO4 7RB.

Test Valley Sporting Guns
35 High Street, Overton, Nr
Basingstoke.
Tel: 0256 770872

Town & Country Sports
19 The Square, Botley.
Tel: 04892 87962

H Cullum (Gunsmiths)
133 Brockhurst Road, Gosort, PO12
3AX.
Tel: 0705 524411

HEREFORD & WORCESTER

C Ashthorpe
Severn Stoke, Worcester, Hereford &
Worcester.

**Astley Redlegged Partridges -
G W Parker & Son**
Astley Burf, Stourport on Severn,
Hereford & Worcester.
Tel: 02993 4593
*Guaranteed to supply only pure red
legged partridges, eggs, chicks,
laying stock.*

Carey (Gunmakers) Ltd
88 The Homend, Ledbury.
Tel: 0531 2838

Davies Baker Gun Co
The Village, Clifton on Teme.

F Durrant & Son
3 Mealcheapen Street, Worcester.
Tel: 0905 25247

G B Sports
120 Broad Street, Ross on Wye.
Tel: 099 63723

Grange Gun Company

Hewell Park, Nr Redditch.
Tel: 0527 46096

M A Ginnal
10 York Street, Stourport on Severn,
Hereford & Worcester
Tel: 029 932212

D Monk Ltd
Unit 32K, Heming Road, Washford
Industrial Estate, Redditch, Hereford
& Worcester.
Tel: 0527 20829

Phillip Morris & Sons
21/23 Widemarsh Street, Hereford.
Tel: 0432 269501

W J Pierce & Son
The Country Gun Shop, Munderfield,
Nr Bromyard, Hereford, HRU 4JU.
Tel: 08853 201

Powells
28 Mount Pleasant, Redditch.
Tel: 0527 62669

**R B Shooting Supplies
Inside Amber Joinery Centre,
Stourport Road, Foley Park,
Kidderminster, Hereford &
Worcester.
Tel: 0562 751159**
*A wide range of clothing and
shooting accessories always in stock
8am to 6pm Monday to Saturday.*

John Slough of London
35 Church Street, Hereford.
Tel: 0432 55416

**Upton Marina Chandlery (Marina
Arms)**
East Waterside, Upton upon Severn,
Hereford & Worcester.
Tel: 06846 3404

**Worcestershire Black Powder
Supplies Ltd**
Units 15/17 Craft Centre,
Wribbenhall, Bewdley, Hereford &
Worcester.
Tel: 0299 402154

Worcestershire Gunsmiths
17/20 New Road, Kidderminster,
Hereford & Worcester.
Tel: 0562 3776

HERTFORDSHIRE

Barhams
95 Tilehouse Street, Hitchin.
Tel: 0462 34298

Bloomfield (Gunmaker)
Hill Farm, Radlett.
Tel: 09276 4639

Duglan & Cooper
Hicks Road, Markyate, St Albans,
Herts.
Tel: 0582 64649

P R Godfrey (Gunsmith)
14 Laxton Gardens, Baldock.
Tel: 0462 892963

The Gun Room (N F Cooper)
50 Hockerhill Street, Bishops
Stortford.
Tel: 0279 52166

Gunner One & Co
1/2 Parkstreet Lane, Parkstreet, St
Albans.
Tel: 0727 72646

Gunshops
15 Cat Hill, East Barnet, Herts.
Tel: 01 441 9594
*Stockists of shotguns, air rifles,
pistols, clothing and a large range of
accessories. North London's largest
gunshop. Closed all Wednesday*

Hertford Guns
31 St Andrews Street, Hertford.
Tel: 0992 553582

Howes and Drage
The Wynd, Letchworth, Herts.
Tel: 0462 674861

Marks Sports Shop
50 Market Street, Watford.
Tel: 0923 39824/50070

Mid Herts Gun Co
2 Mutton Lane, Potters Bar, EN6
2PA
Tel: 0707 43011

T Takats
73 High Street, Ware.
Tel: 0920 2057

HUMBERSIDE NORTH

H H E Akrill (Gunmaker)
18 Market Place, Beverley.

The Cartridge (Beverley)
EYGC Bygot Wood, Cherry Burton,
Beverley.

Duncans (Gunmakers) Ltd
8 Paragon Square, Hull, HU1 3QT.
Tel: 0482 28150

G W Hutchinson Gunmaker
31 Anlaby Road, Hull.
Tel: 0482 223869

Pennine Shooting Centre
Gorrels Way, Rochdale, OL11 2NR.
Tel: 0706 30502

HUMBERSIDE SOUTH

Guns & Tackle
251A Ashby High St,
Scunthorpe.
Tel: 0724 865445
*Prop: Mr J A Bowden
Gun servicing and repairs on all
guns.*

**Humberside Armoury & Angling
Co**
73 Ladysmith Road, Grimsby, South
Humberside.
Tel: 0472 52029

Lightwoods of Grimsby
172 Cleethorpe Road, Grimsby.
Tel: 0472 43536

ISLE OF MAN

G Corlett
6 Castle Street, Douglas.
Tel: 0624 76762

**The Country Gun Shop,
J A Quillam**
Santon Shooting Centre, Ballagick,
Santon
Tel: 0624 74392

Raynors Gun Shop
Murray's Road, Douglas.
Tel: 0624 75706

ISLE OF WIGHT

Arnold Heal Ltd
86B Upper St James Street,
Newport.

Island Gun Centre
26 Birmingham Road, Cowes.
Tel: 0983 299154

KENT

F A Anderson
73a High Street, Ashford, Kent.
Tel: 0233 37717

Jack Laurence Bowes Ltd
4 Third Avenue, Luton, Chatham.
Tel: 0634 407805

T M Dunnell Gunsmith
Rumstead Lane, Stocbury Valley,
Sittingbourne.
Tel: 0795 842200

Gentrys
32/34 Park View Road, Welling.
Tel: 01 304 9922

Don Gray Guns
7 Railway Street, Chatham.
Tel: 0634 43032

H S Greenfield & Son
4/5 Upper Bridge Street, Canterbury.
Tel: 0227 456959

Kent Small Arms
134 High Street, Herne Bay.
Tel: 022 73 64833

Medway Gunrooms Ltd
115 Canterbury Street, Gillingham.
Tel: 0634 576332

Chris Potter Guns
43 Camden Road, Tunbridge Wells.
Tel: 0892 22208

Saddlery and Gun Room, The
368 Main Road, Biggin Hill.
Tel: 0959 73089

A Sanders (Maidstone) Ltd
85 Bank Street, Maidstone.
Tel: 0622 52707

Colin P Smith
61 The Street, Ash, Canterbury.
Tel: 0304 812224

LANCASHIRE

Ballistic Products UK
6 Whitewell, Catterall, Garstang,
Lancs.
Tel: 09952 4251
*UK agent for Ithaca 'Mag Ten'. All
reloading requirements rebarrelling,
sleeving, 4, 8 and 10 bore 'Mag Max'
cartridges, 8, 10 and 12 bore
magnum. Goose shooting trips to
Scotland.*

R Bamford
207 The Green, Eccleston, Nr
Chorley, Lancs, PR7 5PX.
Tel: 0257 451274

Bond & Bywater
42 Fylde Street, Preston, Lancs.
Tel: 0772 58980

S Entwhistle
161 Church Street, Blackpool,
Lancs.
Tel: 0253 20192

S Entwhistle (Preston) Ltd
The Cattle Market, Brook Street,
Preston.

Stephen J Fawcett
7 Gt John Street, Lancaster, LA1
1NQ.
Tel: 0524 32033

Ferrand Custom Arms
Riverside Works, Todmorden Road,
Littleborough, Lancs.
Tel: 0706 78545

Formby Gunshop
9 Three Tuns Lane, Formby,
Merseyside, Lancs, L37 4AG.
Tel: 07048 70598

Ray Fox Guns
48 Bolton Street, Chorley, Lancs.
Tel: 0257 262938

Hiller Airguns & Publications
56 Princes Way, Euxton, Chorley,
Lancs.
Tel: 02572 65489
*Publishers of the collectors guides to
air rifles, Air Pistols and other air gun
books. Send £1.00 for latest 50 page
catalogue.*

**James S Kirkman (Firearms
Dealer)**
12D Blackpool Old Road, Poulton le
Fylde, Lancs.
Tel: 0253 882262/885799

Lancashire Guns
88 Bank Street, Rawtenstall, Lancs.
Tel: 0706 220559

T & J J McAvoy (Guns)
3 High Street, Standish, Wigan,
Lancs.
Tel: Standish 426129

'Macks' Jim Grooby
33a Parliament Street, Burnley,
Lancs.
Tel: 0282 27386

Meggison
8a Main Street, Bolton by Bowland,
Clitheroe, Lancs.
Tel: 02007 602

Pennine Shooting Centre
Gorrels Way, Rochdale, Lancs,
OL11 2NR.
Tel: 0706 30502

Mike Roberts
Park Hill, Garstang, Nr Preston,
Lancs.
Tel: 09952 3925

Shooters Gunroom
56 Darwen Street, Blackburn,

Lancs. Tel: 0254 663547

Target Sports
456 Blackburn Road, Ashley Bridge,
Bolton, Lancs.
Tel: 0204 55513
*The North-West's leading stockist of
air rifles, pistols and crossbows.
Instant credit to bankers and credit
card holders. Access and Visa
accepted. Open six days a week.*

Towers of Rochdale
52 Whitworth Road, Rochdale.
Tel: Rochdale 46171

K Varey
4 New Market Street, Clitheroe,
Lancs.
Tel: 0200 23267

West End Gun Co
18 Alexandra Road, Morecambe.
Tel: 0524 412049

LEICESTERSHIRE

Aylestone Gun Co Ltd
1/3 Paigle Road, Aylestone.
Tel: 0533 832828

Belgrave Gun Co. Ltd.
43 Melton Road, Leicester.
Tel: 0533 663505

**Roger Bolstridge, Sports Guns
& Fishing Tackle**
32 High Street, Coalville.
Tel: 0530 32515

Alan Bray (Guns & Tackle)
5 Waterloo Road, Hinckley, Leics,
LE10 0QJ
Tel: 0455 634317
*Call in for an excellent selection of
shotguns, rifles, pistols, air weapons,
scopes, knives, clothing and many
more accessories.*

**Charnwood Gun & Tackle
(Prop Mr L Jones)**
48 Chapel Street, Ibstock, Leics.
Tel: 0530 60901

Clay Shooters' Supplies
32 St Mary's Road,
Market Harborough.
Tel: 0858 66616

Galway Silencer & Gun Co
2 Old Green, Medbourne Green.
Tel: 085883 706

Ralph Grant & Sons Ltd
Grants Gunroom, Green Lane Road
& Roseberry Street (Off East Park
Road) Leicester.
Tel: 0533 767551

D J Jones
30 Sherrard Street, Melton
Mowbray.

**Loughborough Gun & Angling
Centre**
34 Nottingham Road,
Loughborough, Leics.
Tel: 0509 230627

LINCOLNSHIRE

J Blanch & Son (Gunmakers) Ltd
29 Station Road, Corby Glen,
Grantham, Lincs.
Tel: 047684 628
Gun servicing and repairs

Leslie Bowler Ltd
The Post Office, High Street, Little
Bytham, Grantham, NG33 4QJ.
Tel: 078081 200

P E Charity, The Gun Shop
34 Westgate, Grantham
Tol: 0476 63074

Coppin, Peter
Spinneys Shooting Ground,
Willoughby, Alford, Lincs.
Tel: 0521 22357

Elderkin & Son (Gunmakers) Ltd
17 Broad Street, Spalding.
Tel: 0775 2919/4621

Gun & Tackle Shop
Churchgate, Whaplode, Spalding.

R N & G M Hargrave Gunmakers
9 Market Place, Horncastle,
Lincolnshire.
Tel: 06582 3366

G Harrison & Son
55 Croft Street, Lincoln.
Tel: 0522 23834

**Humberside Armoury & Angling
Co (Gunmakers)**
73 Ladysmith Road, Grimsby.
Tel: 0472 52029/43434

**Lincolnshire Gun Go and Air Gun
Centre**
Eastgate, Louth.
Tel: 0507 603861

R D Marper
Cleatham, Kirton Lindsey,
Gainsborough.
Tel: 0652 648466

Slingsby
19 Westgate, Sleaford.
Tel: 0529 302836

Stamford Gun Room Ltd
8 St Mary's Hill, Stamford.
Tel: 0780 62796
Specialists in antique guns.

J Wheater (Gunmakers) Ltd
3-9 Tentercroft Street, Lincoln.
Tel: 0522 21219

Ian Wilson (Gunmaker)
53 Wide Bargate, Boston.
Tel: 0205 65668

MERSEYSIDE

Merseyside Armoury
83 Lark Lane, Liverpool 17.
Tel: 051 728 8390

Rainford Field Sports
*21 Church St, Rainford, St Helens,
Merseyside.
Tel: Rainford 5580
Shotguns and air rifles bought, sold
or part exchanged. Gun repairs and
a good selection of shooting
accessories. Valumix and Skinners
dogfood.*

Henry Whitty & Son
37/39 School Lane, Liverpool,
L1 3DA.
Tel: 051 709 3011

MIDDLESEX

D & P Guns
33 South Parade, Mollison Way,
Edgware, Middlesex.
Tel: 01 952 1579

Empire Guns
14 Empire Parade, Harrow,
Middlesex.
Tel: 01 807 3802

NORFOLK

Victor Coates Gunsmith
2 Saturday Market Place, Kings
Lynn.
Tel: 0553 763673
*Agents for all leading makes of
shotguns and air rifles. Repairs
carried out on the premises. Wide
range of accessories.*

Darlow & Co (Gunsmiths) Ltd
8 Orford Hill, Norwich.
Tel: 0603 623414

Dereham Gun & Tackle Shop
26 Norwich Street, Dereham.
Tel: 0362 66926

Gallyon & Sons Ltd
9/11 Bedford Street, Norwich.
Tel: 0603 623414

Gun Room The
234 Wroxham Road, Sprowston,
Norwich.
Tel: 0603 49227

J H Ling
Eye Road, Hoxne, Eye.
Tel: 037975 315

Norfolk Gun Trading co
14 Greevegate, Hunstanton.
Tel: 04853 33600

J W Powell (Fakenham) Ltd
5/14 Oak Street, Fakenham.
Tel: 0328 2232

Sporting Guns
London Road, Attleborough,
Norfolk.
Tel: 0953 454506

Uttings Tackle & Gun Shop
54 Bethel Street, Norwich.
Tel: 0603 621776

Woods of Swaffham
7/11 Mangate Street, Swaffham.
Tel: 0760 22609

NORTHAMPTONSHIRE

Brackley Gunsmiths Ltd
95 High Street, Brackley.
Tel: 0280 702519

Peter Crisp Ltd
7 High Street, Rushden.
Tel: 0933 56424

T J Grimley Gunsmith
65 Occupation Road, Corby,
Northants.
Tel: 0536 60719

Northampton Gun Co
136 St James Road, Northampton.
Tel: 0604 51206
*Northampton's only specialist
gunshop, stocking a wide range of
clay and game shooting guns and
accessories, firearms and air rifles.
Full repair service available.*

Sparfield Sporting Guns
19 High Street, Irthlingborough.
Tel: 0933 650296

Sportsman's Lodge
44 Kingsthorpe Road, Northampton.
Tel: 0604 713399

T H Thursby & Son
Sheep Street, Northampton.
Tel: 0604 38225

NORTHUMBERLAND

Game Fair
12 Marygate, Berwick Upon Tweed.
Tel: 0289 305119

T McDermott
112 Station Road, Ashington.
Tel: Ashington 812214

Keith Robson Guns
17 St Mary's Chare, Hexham.
Tel: Hexham 605569

NOTTINGHAMSHIRE

Armstrong's Gunsmiths
360 Carlton Hill, Carlton, Nottingham.
Tel: 0602 873313

Belvoir Shooting Supplies
Orston, Nottinghamshire.
Tel: 0949 50556

Goss Petcher Guns Ltd
The Gun Room, Wighay Bridge,
Annesley Road, Hucknall.
Tel: 0602 633430

Andrew Kay Shooter Supplies
Mount Pleasant Farm, Sturton le
Steeple, Nr Retford.
Tel: 0427 880914

The Nottingham Gun Centre Ltd
155 Attenborough Lane, Beeston.

C Smith & Sons (Newark) Ltd
Clinton House, Lombard Street,
Newark on Trent.
Tel: 0636 703839

OXFORDSHIRE

Banbury Gunsmiths
47a Broad Street, Banbury.
Tel: 0295 65819

Bicester Rod & Gun
9 Kingsley Road, Bicester.
Tel: 0869 241002

R F Bridgman
76 High Street, Witney.
Tel: 0993 2587

Burton & Morgan (Gunsmiths)
The Old Baker, Lower Icknield Way,
Chinnor, Oxford.

Tel: 0844 53655

Casecraft (G H Hawarth)
The Old Telephone Exchange,
Kingston Blount, Nr Oxford.

Cotsworld Guns
Church Street, Charlbury.
Tel: 0608 810891

The Dunmore Shooting Centre
Wootton Road, Abingdon, Oxon.
Tel: 0253 20168
Mike Dingle

The Gun Counter
67 High Street, Wallingford.
Tel: 0491 34343

Hammants
26/28 Bell Street, Henley on
Thames.
Tel: 0491 574545
*Good selection of shotguns, rifles,
air weapons, cartridges, clothing,
knives and shooting accessories
always in stock. Repairs carried out
on our own premises.*

Mark Henshall Country Sports
5/7 Mill Street, Wantage.
Tel: 023 57 2610

John Kent
5/7 Mill Street, Wantage.

Jonathan Lawrence
Park Farm House, Waterstock.
Tel: 08447 469

Thame Shooting Supplies
1st Floor, 15 Cornmarket, Thame,
Oxon.
Tel: 084421 4122

H J Wadley & Son Ltd
30 Market Square, Bicester.

Windrush Guns Ltd
19 Corn Street, Witney, OX8 7DE
Tel: 0993 3035

SHROPSHIRE

Ebrall Brothers
Smithfield Road, Shrewsbury.
Tel: 0743 3048

Gordon Forrest
2 Wyle Cop, Shrewsbury.
Tel: 0743 56878

Guns & Ammo
95 Beatrice Street, Oswestry.
Tel: 0691 653761

Paint & Tool Stores

(Wellington) Ltd
29 New Street, Telford.

A & B Smith
London House, Market Street,
Craven Arms.
Tel: 05882 2368

Sporting & General Supply Co Ltd
1a Swan Hill, Shrewsbury.
Tel: 0743 50991

Herbert Tucker
The Square, Newport, Salop.

Vickers Owen Ltd
Wharf Gun Shop, Mill Street,
Whitchurch, SY13 1SE.
Tel: 0948 2609

W R Wood
Hollydale, Buildwas Road,
Iron Bridge.

SOMERSET

Bridgwater Guns Ltd
22 St Mary Street, Bridgwater.
Tel: 0278 423441

Dan-Arm (UK) Ltd
Unit 7, Hortonwood 33, Telford,
Shropshire, TF1 4EX.
Tel: 0952 608047

Denton & Kennell
West Street, Somerton.
Tel: 0458 73732/72065

The Flintlock
17A High Street, Glastonbury.
Tel: 0458 31225

Lance Nicholson Fishing & Guns
High Street, Dulverton.
Tel: 0398 23409

Neroche Armoury
Rose Mill, Hort Bridge, Ilminster.
Tel: 0460 53722

Frank Richards
25 Silver Street, Taunton.
Tel: 0823 81487

Sherwood Guns & Cartridges
Littlemore Road, Mark, Nr Highbridge
Tel: 027864 419

Shotgun Supplies
Lower Odcombe, Yeovil.
Tel: 093 586 2712

That Tackle Shop
29 Princes Street, Yeovil.
Tel: 0935 74600

Wesley Hamm

Winchester Farm, Wells Road,
Cheddar.
Tel: 0934 742563

The Willows Gunshop
Lilylane, Templecombe, Somerset,
BA8 0HN.
Tel: 0963 70129
*A large selection of shotguns,
Cartridges, Waxproofs, Socks,
Sweaters, Bodywarmers, Moleskins,
Aigle Wellingtons. Full overhauling
and repair service. Specialists in
leather skeet vests.*

STAFFORDSHIRE

G Bate (Gunmakers) Ltd
7 Market Square, Stafford.
Tel: 0785 44191

John Birks (Sports)
293 Uttoxeter Road, Normacott,
Stoke on Trent, ST3 5LQ.

Thomas Blakemore
Excelsior Works, Bath Street,
Walsall.

G R Bourne (Guns & Tackle)
40 King Street, Newcastle.
Tel: 0782 625385

Catton Gunsmiths
Catton Hall, Burton on Trent,
DE12 5LN.

Tom Cooper
Hanley Gunshop Ltd, 28-30 Pall
Mall, Hanley, Stoke on Trent.
Tel: 0782 281589

**R E Garland, Garlands Shooting
Ground**
Edingale, Nr Tamworth.
Tel: 082 785300

J M Green Guns & Tackle
42 Crewe Road, Alsager, Stoke on
Trent.
Tel: 09363 2983

**Lakefield Armoury Company
Limited**
1/3 Church Street, Audley, Stoke on
Trent, ST7 8DE.
Tel: 0782 722257
*Black powder, replica weapon
specialists of long establishment.*

Lichfield Gun Co
13 Lyn Avenue, Lichfield, Staffs,
WS13 7DA.
Tel: 0543 262416

M B Guns
Rear 187 Waterloo Street, Burton
on Trent.
Tel: 0283 32479

**Morlands Shotgun Supplies
(Prop R M Blythe)**
3 Lightoaks Level, Oakamoor.

Practical Weaponry
162 Bucknall New Road, Hanley,
Stoke on Trent.
Tel: 0782 29712

Wm Riley & Sons Ltd
High Street, Halmer End, Stoke on
Trent.
Tel: 0782 720212

Rugeley Guns & Tackle
5 Market Square, Rugeley.
Tel: 08894 79002

**Specialist Military Sales
(Prop Mr P Bark)**
109 Hednesford Road, Heath
Hayes.

Willenhall Airgun Supplies
3 Pross Street, Willonhall, Staffs.
Tel: 0902 633000
*Full range of air rifles, accessories,
cartridges. Open 6 days a week.
Closed Sun. Access & Barclaycard
welcome.*

SUFFOLK

Abbott's Rod and Gun Shop
18 Church Street, Woodbridge,
Suffolk.
Tel: Suffolk 2377
*Specialist repairs undertaken also
fishing tackle and baits. Many
shotguns & air rifles in stock at all
times. Access & Barclaycard
welcome.*

Alfred Clark
69 St Matthews Street, Ipswich.
Tel: 0473 52498

Anglia Arms
96 Risbygate Street, Bury St
Edmunds.
Tel: 0284 61470

R M & D Clayton
Town Hall Gun Works, 4a The
Traverse, Bury St Edmunds.
Tel: 0284 4559

Coach Harness
Haughley, Stowmarket, Suffolk,

IP14 3NS.
Tel: 0449 673258
Mail order only.

East Coast Gunroom
29 Beach Station road, Felixstowe,
IP11 8DR.
Tel: 0394 282100

Morgan Guns Ltd
Eurosports Village, Shotley Gate, Nr
Ipswich.
Tel: Shotley 717/740

A Richardson & Sons (Gunsmiths)
32 Quay Street, Halesworth.
Tel: 09867 2520

Rod & Gun Shop
18 Church Street, Woodbridge.
Tel: 039 43 2377

Suffolk Gun Club
42/44 Upper Orwell Street, Ipswich.
Tel: 0473 210914

R Tilney (Gunsmith)
17 Small Gate, Beccles.
Tel: 0502 712105

SURREY

A E Clarke & Co (Yateley) Ltd
55 London Road, Blackwater,
Camberley.
Tel: 0276 35616
Manufacturers AEC rifle sights.

**Cranleigh Field Sports,
(Gunsmiths)**
Ewhurst Road, Cranleigh.
Tel: 0483 272071

Dees Sports
7 Manor Road, Wallington, SM6 0BZ
Tel: 01 647 7742

**Dorking Gun Company
(Gunmakers)**
243a High Street, Dorking,
RH4 1RT.
Tel: 0306 883451

Egham Gun Centre
83 High Street, Egham.
Tel: 0784 33424

Farnham Saddlers
7 West Street, Farnham.
Tel: 0252 713004

Jeffreys of Guilford
134 High Street, Guildford.
Tel: 0483 505055

Masters Gunmakers Ltd
Cannon Works, Ockley Road, Beare

Green, Dorking, RH5 4PU.
Tel: 0306 711435

John Powell Gunmakers
45 Church Street, Reigate.
Tel: 073 72 44111

Surrey Guns Ltd
9 Manor Road, Wallington.
Tel: 01 647 0017

Andrew Tucker Ltd
58 Portsmouth Road, Cobham,
Surrey, KT11 1HY.
Tel: 0932 62921

Walton Tackle Shop
166 Station Road, Addlestone.
Tel: 0932 42528

Ray Ward
41 Holland Close, Redhill, RH1 1RT.
Tel: 0737 66715

Richard Wells (Sporting Guns)
The Gun Shop, Lionmead,
Shottermill, Haslemere, GU27 3NH.
Tel: 0428 51913

Weybridge Guns & Tackle Ltd
180 Oatlands Drive, Weybridge,
KT13 9ET
Tel: 0932 42675

SUSSEX EAST

F A Anderson
12 East Street, Brighton.
Tel: Brighton 23066

The Armoury Nappers
High Street, Mayfield, TN20 6AB.
Tel: 0435 873288

Diamond Guns
67 High Street, Heathfield.
Tel: 042 52 3295

Hestons
37 Coombe Terrace, Brighton.
Tel: 0273 693248

S A Lambert (Gunsmith)
5 Friarshill Terrace, Guestling,
Hastings.
Tel: 0424 813299

Lewes Gun Room
127 High Street, Lewes.
Tel: Lewes 474669
Gunsmiths

Sussex Guns
203 Preston Road, Brighton.
Tel: 0273 553222

D Townsend (Gunsmiths)
63 Preston Street, Brighton.
Tel: 0273 25245

Wisdens (G Hastings) Ltd
1 Trinity Street, Hastings.
Tel: 0424 421240

SUSSEX WEST

Anscombe & Hall
2 Caudle Street, Henfield.
Tel: Henfield 494340

Chichester Armoury, The
43 West Street, Chichester.
Tel: 0243 774687

Churchley Brothers Ltd
282 Goring Road, Worthing.
Tel: 0903 46301

The Covert
34 East Street, Petworth, West
Sussex.
Tel: 0798 43118

Horsham Gun Shop
42 East Street, Horsham.
Tel: 0403 52684

Kirkman (Crawley) Ltd
Starway Nurseries, Copthorne
Common, Crawley, RH10 3JU.
Tel: 0293 26670

Michael Miller
The Lamb, 8 Cuckfield Road,
Hurstpierpoint.
Tel: 0273 834567

Selous Hunters
Horsted Keynes, W Sussex,
RH17 7AJ.
Tel: 0825 790834
*Selous Hunters Professional African
Hunters and Safari Outfitters
supplying fine Antique and Modern
Sporting Guns and Rifles for
discerning sportsmen and collectors.
Full Gunsmithing, Fine Rifles made
to order. Regularly visiting
international clients in Europe and
America. Visits to premises by
appointment only.*

Sports & Radio
25/29 Aldwick Road, Bognor Regis.

Sussex Gun Room
The Covert, East Street, Petworth.
Tel: 0798 43118

Craig M Whitsey (Gunmakers) Ltd
Unit D, 10/12 Fitzalan Road,

Arundel, W Sussex.
Tel: 0903 883102

Worthing Gun Shop
80 Broadwater Street West,
Worthing.
Tel: 0903 37378

TYNE & WEAR

Bagnall & Kirkwood Ltd
52 Grey Street, Newcastle.
Tel: 0632 325875

P Bradford Stalker Firearms
Ouston Bank farm, Ouston, Chester
le Street, DH2 1BB.
Tel: 091 4100565
Bereta Custom Grade Dealer

Caer Urfa Guns and Ammo
399 Stanhope Road, South Shields.
Tel: 0632 551045

Coast & Country Sports
3 Derwent Street, Sunderland.
Tel: 0783 659666

The County House
123/125 Clayton Street West,
Newcastle-upon-Tyne.
Tel: 0632 616669

J R Murdy
Unit 15, Swan Road, Swan Ind Est,
District 9, Washington.

K9 Tackle & Guns
21a Derwent Street, Sunderland,
Tyne & Wear.
Tel: 0783 674378
*Walking sticks, hats, caps, scarves,
stockings, bodywarmers, jackets,
ties moleskin trousers, moleskin
shirts. Uniroyal shooters & waders.
Agents for House of Hardy
Countrywear.*

Steve Smith Gunmaker
37 Nelson Street, Newcastle-upon-
Tyne.
Tel: 0632 322776

Pat Walker Guns
143 Alexandra Road, Gateshead.
Tel: 0632 786736

WARWICKSHIRE

Astwood Guns
4 High Street, Strudley.
Tel: 052 785 4963

Cartridge, The
16 Smith Street, Warwick.
Tel: 0926 491087

Guns & Sports
26 Henley Street, Stratford Upon
Avon.
Tel: 0789 67100

Gun Shop, The
62a Lawford Road, Rugby.
Tel: 0788 751198

Hogan & Colbourne Gunmakers
Phoenix Works, Alscot Park,
Stratford Upon Avon.
Tel: 078987 764

Sidelock Guns
1a Coleshill Road, Atherstone.
Tel: 08277 2903

WEST MIDLANDS

Accles & Shelvoke Ltd
Palford Street, Aston, Birmingham 6.
Tel: 021 359 3277

Bailons Gunmakers Ltd
94/95 Bath Street, Birmingham.
Tel: 021 236 7593

G Bate (Gunmakers) Ltd
8/10 Colmore Circus, Birmingham.
Tel: 021 236 7451

A A Brown & Sons
1 Snake Lane, Alvechurch,
Birmingham.
Tel: 021 445 5395
*Secondhand English shotguns
usually available. Apply for list.*

City Air Weapons & Firearms
260 Lyndon Road, Olton, Solihull.
Tel: 021 742 1329

William Ford Ltd
352 Moseley Road, Birmingham,
B12 9AZ.
Tel: 021 440 3233

Godiva Guns (Coventry)
191 Canley Road, Coventry,
CV5 6AS.
Tel: 0203 76077

Peter Gordon
84 High Street, Dudley.
Tel: 0384 52413

W W Greener Ltd
Belmont Row, Birmingham.
Tel: 021 359 5757

Highfield Gun Co Ltd
158 Highfield Road, Hall Green,
Birmingham, B28 0HT.
Tel: 021 778 5465

William Howell
63 Price Street, Birmingham.
Tel: 021 359 3452

JLS Arms Co Ltd
Scoltock House, Perry Street,
Wednesbury.
Tel: 021 556 9658
Telex: 333245 JLSARM/G

Clive C Lemon Gunmaker
Malt Mill Lane, Halesowen, West
Midlands.
Tel: 021 559 5717

G E Lewis & Sons
32/33 Lower Loveday Street,
Birmingham.
Tel: 021 359 2750/0789 750475

J Manton & Co Ltd
140 Bromsgrove Street, Birmingham,
B6 6RQ.

Alfred J Parker
348 Moseley Road, Birmingham 12
Tel: 021 440 1480

**William Powell & Son (Gunmaker)
Ltd**
35/37 Carrs Lane, Birmingham.
Tel: 021 643 0689/8362

Salisburys Gunsmiths
32a Lower Loveday Street,
Birmingham.
Tel: 021 359 7362

**C H Smith & Sons (Gunmakers)
Ltd.**
63 Price Street, Birmingham 4.
Tel: 021 359 1680

**Frank Spittle (Guns) & (Martial
Arts)**
216 Bushbury Road, Fallings Park,
Wolverhampton.
Tel: 0902 731383

Trapshot
Unit 13 Mucklow Enterprise Estate,
Pedmore Road, Brierley Hill.
Tel: 0384 265151

Turner Richards
Cardigan Street, Birmingham,
B4 7SA.
Tel: 021 359 5577

Venom Arms Co
Unit 1, Gun Barrel Ind Centre,
Hayseech Road, Cradley Heath,
Warley.
Tel: 021 501 3794

Rowland Watson

32 Lower Loveday Street,
Birmingham.
Tel: 021 359 1830

Wednesbury Marksmen
Rifle & Pistol Range, Perry Street,
Wednesbury, West Midlands.
Tel: 021 556 1322
Handgun and accessories specialists.

Westley Richards & Co Ltd
40 Grange Road, Bournebrook,
Birmingham.
Tel: 021 472 1701

Wiseman Gunmakers
262 Walsall Road, Bridgtown,
Crannock, WS1 13JL
Tel: 05435 4088

WILTSHIRE

Barbury Guns Ltd
44/45 High Street, Marlborough,
SN8 1HQ.
Tel: 0672 52862

The Fieldsman
10 Rodbourne Road, Swindon.

Greenfield of Salisbury Ltd
21 Milford Street, Salisbury.
Tel: 0722 333795/6

Chris Harding Guns
Cresswell Lane, Lea, Malmesbury.
Tel: 06662 2447

Limmex Field Sports
High Street and Wood Street, Old
Town, Swindon.
Tel: 0793 22056

Kenlis R Ponting
Tadpole Farm, Blunsdon, Swindon.
Tel: 0793 770305

Westbury Guns
12 Edwards Street, Westbury, Wilts,
BA1 3BD.
Tel: 0373 826081
*High class stockists of all leading
accessories and coaching facilities.
Excellent selection of Browning,
Beretta etc. Repair and alteration
service available.*

Wiltshire Rod & Gun
23 High Street, Old Town, Swindon.
Tel: 0793 47455

Wiltshire Shooting Centre
Station Road, Devizes.
Tel: 0380 77282

Wiltshire Smallarms Company
PO Box 36, Devizes, Wiltshire, .
SN10 1UZ.
Tel: 0380 6610
*Retailer and wholesaler of 20th
century smallarms and ammunition.*

YORKSHIRE NORTH

Messrs J Anderson & Son
4 Saville Street, Malton.
Tel: 0653 2367

Barrington C Davies
4/6 Cheltenham Parade, Harrogate.
Tel: 0423 505677

Bulmers Gunsmiths
1/7 Lord Mayors Walk, York.
Tel: 0904 20788

The Cartridge (Beverley)
EYGC Bygot Wood, Cherry Burton,
Beverley.

Cawood Gun Co
Sherburn Street, Cawood, Nr Selby.
Tel: 075 786 223

John Gretton Shooting & Fishing
28 Northway, Scarborough.
Tel: 0723 368771
*Comprehensive range of shotguns,
air rifles, full and small bore rifles
and pistols. New and secondhand.
Part exchange welcome. Full repair
service – restocking a speciality.*

The Gun Room
Leeds Road, Huddersfield, West
Yorkshire.

Gun Shop, The (Otley) Ltd
36 Cross Green, Pool Road, Otley.
Tel: 0943 462770

Hargers for Guns
Cheapside, Settle.
Tel: 07292 3751

R G Hodgson
7 Queen Street, Ripon.
Tel: 0765 3029

Hookes of York Ltd
28/30 Coppergate, York.
Tel: 0904 55073

John A Jackson
9/10 Queen Street, Scarborough.
Tel: 0723 360904

**Linsley Bros Ltd (Barrington C
Davies)**
4/6 Cheltenham Parade, Harrogate.
Tel: 0423 55677

W Metcalf & Son
5 Market Place, Richmond.
Tel: 0748 2108

R J & B Morley
7 Bishopsthorpe Road, York.
Tel: 0904 23007

Shooting Lodge, The
29/30 Victoria Street, Skipton
Tel: 0756 5825

P H & J R Smith
28 High Street, Knaresborough,
N Yorks.
Tel: 0423 863322

Thirsk Gunrooms
4 Finkle Street, Thirsk, N Yorks.
Tel: 0845 24355

York Guns
9 King Street, York.
Tel: 0904 31913

Yorkshire Airweapons
209 Stanningley Road, Leeds 12,
Yorkshire.
Tel: 0532 798039
*Yorkshire's leading stockists of air
rifles, pistols and crossbows. Instant
credit to bankers and credit card
holders. Access and visa accepted.
Open 6 days a week.*

Yorkshire Gun Room
35/37 Swan Road, Harrogate,
N Yorks.
Tel: 0423 61182

Yorkshire Gun Room
4 Finkle Street, Thirsk.
Tel: 0845 24355

YORKSHIRE SOUTH

Doncaster Shooters Supply Ltd
12 Copley Road, Doncaster.
Tel: 0302 67615

Exelair Shooting Club
346 Sheffield Road, Birdwell,
Barnsley.
Tel: 0226 748629/744490

Field Sports Supplies
YMCA Buildings, 10 Pitt Street,
Barnsley.
Tel: 0226 206326

Guns International
502 Doncaster Road, Stairfoot,
Barnsley.
Tel: 0226 289155

Gunsport
125 Wellgate, Rotherham.
Tel: 0709 377406

Hardy's Gunsmiths
367 Eccleshall Road, Sheffield.
Tel: 0742 668403

Northern Arms Co
62b Copley Road, Doncaster.
Tel: 0302 60265

Arthur Turner (Sheffield) Ltd
33-35 West Bar, Sheffield, S3 8PQ.
Tel: 0742 24602

George Wood & Co Ltd
113/115 Pinstone Street, Sheffield.
Tel: 0742 23334

YORKSHIRE WEST

B & I Bancer
18 Pontefract Road, Castleford.
Tel: 0977 554339

Carters of Bradford Ltd
15 Bridge Street, Bradford.
Tel: 0274 726215

The Castle Air Gun Centre
6 Castle Way, Castleford.
Tel: 0977 511452

Dobson & Robinson
46 The Grove, Ilkey, W Yorks,
LS29 9EE.
Tel: 0943 608549

Peter Dyson Ltd
31 Church Street, Honley,
Huddersfield.
Tel: 0484 661062

R E Heathcote-Walker
The Cottage, Gomersal House,
Lower Lane, Gomersal, BD19 4HY.
Tel: 0274 877498

A J Jewson
1 Westgate, Halifax, W Yorks.
Tel: 0422 541146
*Guns & fishing tackle. Cartridges
Eley 'Nike', clay pigeons. Wide range
of guns, air pistols, rifles, shotguns.*

Richard Jones
7 Horsefair, Wetherby, LS22 4JG.
Tel: 0937 65919

J P S Guns
22 Lower Warrengate, Wakefield.
Tel: 0924 379215

Kirklees Gun Shop
17 Lord Street, Huddersfield.
Tel: 0484 44600

Henry Krank & Co Ltd
108 Lowtown, Pudsey.
Tel: 0532 569163/0532 565167

**Linsley Brothers Ltd (Barrington C
Davies)**
28 Kirkgate, Leeds LS2 7DR.
Tel: 0532 452790

**J S Ramsbottom – Park Lane
Service Station**
Park Lane, Keighley.
Tel: 0535 605445

Pennine Shooting Centre
Manorley Lane, Bradford.
Tel: 0274 603665

**Pennington's Sporting Arms &
Ammunition**
67 Bridge St, Castleford, West
Yorkshire.

Pheasant Valley Shooting Range
Unit 6, Tower Works, Globe Road,
Leeds, West Yorkshire, LS11 5QG.
Tel: 0532 460003

**B G Pollard, Thornhill Armourers
Shop**
88 Thornhill Street, Calverley,
Leeds.
Tel: 0532 568356

David J Rimington
Rathwell, Leeds
Tel: 0532 822540

Sambrook Shooting Sports
180 Leeds Road, Newton Hill,
Wakefield.
Tel: 0924 365384

Silsden Sporting Guns
31 Skipton Road; Silsden, Nr
Keighley.
Tel: 0535 56058

**Swillington Shooting & Stable
Supplies**
Home Farm, Wakefield Road, Leeds.
Tel: 0532 864097

Yorkshire Air Weapons
209 Stanningley Road, Armley,
Leeds.

SCOTLAND

BORDERS

Country Gun Shop, The
Lilliesleaf, Melrose, Roxburghshire,
TD6 9JD.
Tel: 083 57315

Established 1966. Proprietor Mr A Walter. Closed Mondays. Suppliers of sporting guns, rifles and pistols. Also accessories, including our own custom loaded Eildon cartridges. Gun repairs by skilled craftsmen.

John Dickson & Son
35 The Square, Kelso.
Tel: 0573 24687

Ian Fraser Sports
1 Bridgegate, Peebles.
Tel: 0721 20979

Game and Country Enterprises
6-8 Cannon Gate, Jedburgh,
Roxburghshire.

R Welsh & Son
28 Castle Street, Duns, TD11 3D.
Tel: 0361 83466

CENTRAL

D Crockhart & Son
15 King Street, Stirling, FK8 1DN.
Tel: 0786 73443
The friendly shop with the big reputation. Shotguns, rifles, air weapons, ammunition, clothing and accessories including small bore. Second hand weapons, bought and sold.

Glasgow Range Supplies Ltd
6 Main Street, Menstrie.
Tel: 0259 61301

Isles & Macrae (Guns & Ammo)
5 Friars Street, Stirling.
Tel: 0786 62182
For all your shooting and fishing needs. Full range of shotguns, Webley airguns, scopes, slings. All makes of cartridges. Good selection of replicas, holsters, shoulder holster. Live bait seven days a week. Special discounts for clubs.

J K Angling & Guns
101 Mary Square, Laurieston,
Falkirk, FK2 9PR.
Tel: 0324 23156

Alex Martin
20 Royal Exchange Square,
Glasgow.

McLaren's of Bridge Allen
4 Allanvale Road, Bridge of Allen,
FK9 4NU.

DUMFRIES & GALLOWAY

Castle Douglas Guns & Tackle
9 St Andrews Street, Castle
Douglas.
Tel: 0556 2977

Clickety Click
67 High Street, Lockerbie.
Tel: 05762 2400

M McCowan & Son
41/43 High Street, Dalbeattie,
DG5 4AN.

M McCowan & Son
50-52 King Street, Castle Douglas,
DG7 1AE.
Tel: 0556 2009

Pattie's of Dumfries
109 Queensberry Street, Dumfries,
DG1 1BH.
Tel: 0387 52891

Solway Shooting Supplies
8 The Green, Eastriggs, Annan.

The Gun Shop
40 Queen Street, Newton Stewart,
Wigtownshire.
Tel: 0671 2570

The Post Office
The Green, Eastriggs.
Tel: 04614 201

FIFE

Fife Field Sports
Windygates, Fife.
Tel: 0333 351458

Hamblet Ltd
t/a Country Sports, St Andrew
Street, Dumfermline, Fife,
KY11 4QG.
Tel: 0383 729546

John A Stewart
31 Ladywynd, Cupar, KY15 4DE.

Were Game

GRAMPIAN

Anderson Guns
201 Hardgate, Aberdeen, AB1 2YP.
Tel: 0224 201179

Country Ways
115 Holburn Street, Aberdeen,
Aberdeenshire, AB1 6BQ.
Tel: 0224 585150
Saddlers & field sports outfitters. Country Wear by Barbour, Bladen, Hardy, Bridgedale, Puffa, Beaver.

Shooting accessories, picnic baskets, lunch bags, spirit flasks, prints and books.

Countrywear
15 & 35 Bridge Street, Ballater, Aberdeenshire.
Tel: 0338 55453

Grampian Guns
Ravensmead, Newmachar, Aberdeen, AB5 0PU.
Tel: 06517 2273

R M Jeffries
39 New Street, Rothes.
Tel: 034 03 407

Macsport Ltd
4 Bridge Street, Banchory.
Tel: 03302 2855

George D Manson
45 Gordon Street, Huntly.
Tel: 0466 2482

Robertson Sports
1/3 Kirk Street, Peterhead, Aberdeenshire.

HIGHLANDS & ISLANDS

J Graham & Co Ltd
71 Castle Street, Inverness.
Tel: 0463 233178

Gray & Co Gunmakers
30 Union Street, Inverness.
Tel: 0463 233225

Robert H Hall (Guns)
Willowburn Road, Kirkwall, Orkney.
Tel: 0856 2880

C H Haygarth & Sons
The Cottage Gun Shop, The Dunnet, Caithness, KW14 8HQ.
Tel: 084 785602

Knox House
Shore Road, Brodick, Isle of Arran.
Tel: 0770 2416

Leisuropa Ltd
6/8 Inglis Street, Inverness.
Tel: 04632 39427

MacLean Sports
33 High Street, Dingwall, Ross-shire.
Tel: 0349 63147

R Macleod & Son
14 Lamington Street, Tain, Ross-shire.
Tel: 0862 2171
Beretta custom grade dealers.

G C Mortimer & Son
61 High Street, Grantown on Spey.
Tel: 0479 2684
Send £1 for lists of second hand shotguns, rifles, revolvers and pistols.

Ormiston & Co
Market Brae Steps, Inverness.
Tel: 0463 222757

Rod & Gun Shop
68 High Street, Fort William.
Tel: 0397 2656

Rob Wilson Rod & Guns
Brora
Tel: 0408 21373

Wilson & Nolf
1 Francis Street, Wick, KW1 5PZ.
Tel: 0955 4284

Wilson & Nolf
28/29 Breadalbane Terrace, Wick.

ISLE OF SKYE

A Hodgson
4 Luib, Broadford.

LOTHIAN

Country Life
229 Balgreen Road, Edinburgh.
Tel: 031 337 6230

John Dickson & Son
21 Frederick Street, Edinburgh, EH2 2NE.
Tel: 031 225 4218

Edinburgh Gun Makers
73 Rose Street, Edinburgh.
Tel: 031 225 2641

Field & Stream Ltd
61 Montrose Terrace, Edinburgh, EH7 5DP.
Tel: 031 661 4282

Shooting Lines Ltd
23 Roseburn Terrace, Edinburgh, EH12 5NG.
Tel: 031 337 8616

F & D Simpson
28 West Preston Street, Edinburgh, EH8 9PZ.

David Taylor
Tel: 031 332 4873

M B Thompson & Son
19 East London Street, Edinburgh.
Tel: 031 556 5682

STRATHCLYDE

Alexander Dalgleish
11 Montgomery Street, Eaglesham,
Glasgow, G76 0AS.
Tel: 03553 3595

Crocket, The Ironmonger Ltd
136 West Hill Street, Glasgow.
Tel: 041 332 1041

Gamesport
60 Sandgate, Ayr, KA7 1BX.
Tel: 0292 263822

Guns & Tackle
25 Portland Place, Hamilton.
Tel: 0698 422904
Shotguns, firearms, air rifles and
pistols, shooting accessories, new
and second hand guns. Part
exchange on all weapons. Prompt
gun servicing and repairs. Open Mon
to Sat 9.00–5.30.

James Kirk Tackle & Guns
Union Arcade, Ayre.
Tel: 0292 263390

Pat Loughrin
54-56 Caledonian Road, Wishaw.
Tel: 0698 374513

John Dickson & Son
20 Royal Exchange Square,
Glasgow.
Tel: 041 221 6794

McCririck & Sons
38 John Finnie Street, Kilmarnock.
Tel: 0563 25577

D McKay-Brown Gunmaker
32 Hamilton Road, Bothwell,
Glasgow, G71 8NA.
Tel: 0698 853727

Pitchers Sports
23 Moss Street, Paisley.
Tel: 041 889 6969

Richardson Sports
Shopping Hall 2, Salvanna Way,
Clydebank.

Tackle & Guns
918 Pollockshaws Road, Glasgow,
G41 2ET.
Tel: 041 632 2733

Ian Tyrell Guns
165 High Street, Dumbarton.
Tel: 0389 34438

TAYSIDE

Angus Gun Room & Fishing

Tackle Centre
98 Ferry Road, Dundee.
Tel: 0382 453668

James Crockart & Son
26 Allan Street, Blairgowrie,
PH10 6AD.
Tel: 0250 2056

John R Gow & Sons
12 Union Street, Dundee, DD1 4BH.
Tel: 0382 25427

W R Hardy Gunsmith
153 East High Street, Forfar.
Tel: 0307 66635

Highland Gathering
Pitlochry.
Tel: 0796 3047

Highlands Guns & Tackle
Blair Athol.
Tel: 079681 303

Kerr of Crieff
36 James Square, Crieff.
Tel: 0764 1659
Suppliers of sporting guns and
pistols, accessories, wide range of
clothing and footwear. Gun repairs
undertaken.

MG Guns & Tackle
51 York Place, Perth.
Tel: 0738 25769
We stock a complete range of
shooting and fishing accessories at
excellent rates. Also firearms,
shotguns, deer stalking and our own
shooting school. Open 8.30–6.00
Mon-Sat.

W Phillips
180 High Street, Montrose.
Tel: 0674 72692

Shotcast Ltd
8 Whitehall Crescent, Dundee,
DD1 4AU
Tel: 0382 25621

Sporting Guns & Ammo
55 North Methven Street, Perth.
Tel: 0738 23679

P D Malloch
259 Old High Street, Perth.
Tel: 0738 32316

WALES

CLWYD

Fieldsports Equipe

20a Elwy Street, Rhyl, Flintshire, LL18.

Harry's Tackle
Unit 20, Queens Supermarket, High Street, Rhyl.
Tel: 0745 54765

North Wales Shooting School
Sealand Manor, Sealand, Chester.
Tel: 0244 812219

R D Pickering & Son
60 Abergele Road, Colwyn Bay.
Tel: 0492 2551

Rucksack 'N' Rifle
12 Abbot Street, Wrexham, Clwyd, LL11 1TA.
Tel: 0978 350553

The Shooting Sports Co
36 Lambpit Street, Wrexham, Clwyd.
Tel: 0978 359009

Strathyre Armoury
Darland Lane, Rossett, Wrexham, Clwyd.
Tel: 097883 2550

DYFED

Aber Guns & Tackle
13 Terrace Road, Aberystwyth, SY23 1NY.
Tel: 0970 3340

Anglers Corner
65 Robinson Street, Llanelli, SA15 1TT

Consumer Technical Supplies 'Efailfach'
Llanfair, Clydogau, Lampeter, SA48 8LG.

County Sports
3 Old Bridge, Haverfordwest.
Tel: 0437 3740

G T Griffiths
Teifi Valley Shooting Supplies, Llechryd, Cardigan.
Tel: 023987 204

Llanfair Gunshop
Llanfair Clydogau, Lampeter.
Tel: 057045 356

L J Williams & Son, Gun Dealers
Garth, Llanrhystyd, SY23 5DQ.

GLAMORGAN MID

Coed Y Brain
4 Bartlett Street, Caerphilly.
Tel: 0222 882802

Country Gunshop, The
100 Penprysg Road, Pencoed, Nr Bridgend, CF35 6LT.
Tel: 0656 860252

Keen's Tackle & Guns
97 Bridgend Road, Aberkenfig, Nr Bridgend, Mid Glamorgan, South Wales, CF32 9AP.
Tel: 0656 722448
For all your shooting and fishing requirements.

Lloyds
40 Canon Street, Aberdare, CF44 7A.
Tel: 0685 873717

GLAMORGAN SOUTH

A Bale & Sons Ltd
3 Frederick Street, Cardiff.
Tel: 0222 29929

Countryside Promotions, Neath Gun Shop
44 Briton Ferry Road, Neath.

Crown House Armoury Ltd
Cogan Hill, Windsor Road, Penarth.
Tel: 0222 706181

Lakeside Guns (Prop R S Schulz)
4 Dynevor Road, Cyncoed, Cardiff, CF37 HZ.

GLAMORGAN WEST

Lewis Sports
64 Commercial Road, Port Talbot.
Tel: 0639 882312

West Wales Gun Co
6 James Street, Pontardawe.
Tel: 0792 863181

GWENT

H H Keeling & Sons
48 Monnow Street, Monmouth, NP5 3EN.

D J Litt (Firearms) Ltd
Unit 3, Maesglas Ind Estate, Newport.
Tel: 0633 50025

Herbert Tucker
The Square, Newport, Shropshire.

GWYNED

Angling & Gun Centre
11/13 High Street, Porthmadog.
Tel: 0766 2464

Gwynedd Firearms

99 High Street, Bangor.
Tel: 0248 351641

W E Pugh Sports Dealer
74 High Street, Bala.
Tel: 0678 520248

POWYS

N J Guns (Prop Mr N Jones)
2A High Street, Builth Wells.
Tel: 0982 552174

Roberts & Quin
Commercial Street, Newtown.
Tel: 0686 26579

A W Weale (Gunsmith)
Trebowen, Talgarth, LD3 0BB.
Tel: 0874 711 443

NORTHERN IRELAND

ANTRIM

C F Beatie
66 Main Street, Ballycarry,
BT38 9HH.
Tel: 09603 72462

Hugh Craig & Sons
16 The Square, Ballyclare, B39 9BD.
Tel: 09603 22329

Lisburn Sports Centre
9 Smithfield Square, Lisburn,
BT28 1TH.
Tel: 09462 77975

James Matthews
72 Ballymoney Street, Ballymena,
BT43 6A.

Kenneth Rankin Ltd
131 Royal Avenue, Belfast,
BT1 1FG.

Spence Bros
32 New Street, Randalstown,
BT41 3AF.
Tel: 08494 72248

ARMAGH

T H Lavery
56 Clonmakate Road, Birches,
Portadown, BT62.
Tel: 0762 851215

Victor Mateer
7 Main Street, Donaghcloney,
Craigavon, Co Armagh.
Tel: 0762 881235

CO DOWN

Joseph Bradell & Son Ltd

9 North Street, Belfast, BT1 1AN.
Tel: 320525

John M Clegg & Co Ltd
48 Regent Street, Newtownards,
BT23 4LP.
Tel: 0247 812585

Comber Sports Centre Ltd
18 Castle Street, Comber,
BT23 5DZ.
Tel: 0247 872846

Hollow Farm Shooting Grounds
35 Drumkirk Road, Comber, Co
Down.
Tel: 0238 528381

John C Smyth
5/7 Kildare Street, Newry, BT34.
Tel: 0693 5303

**B A Thompson Firearms
Unlimited**
463 Gransha Road, Bangor,
BT19 2PX.

Traps & Tackle
6 Seacliff Road, Bangor, Co Down.
Tel: 0247 458515

FERMANAGH

Lakeland Tackle
Sligo Road, Enniskillen.
Tel: 0365 23774

LONDONDERRY

H Burke & Son
11 Quilly Road, Coleraine, BT52.

H Burke & Son
70-76 Long Commons, Coleraine.
Tel: Coleraine 2804/3496 after 6pm

J A McGuigan
95 Main Street, Maghera,
BT46 5AB.

Smyth Bros
15 Church Street, Coleraine,
BT52 1A.
Tel: 0265 52957

J C Stewart
1/2 Union Road, Magherafelt,
BT45 5DA.
Tel: 0648 32392

TYRONE

Field & Stream
30 Killyman Street, Moy,
Dungannon, Co Tyrone.
Tel: 08687 84556

S Kyles & Sons
Fivemiletown, Co Tyrone.
Tel: 03655 21207

M C Vey Bros
49/51 Molesworth Street,
Cookstown, BT80 8NX.
Tel: 024 92026

REPUBLIC OF IRELAND

Cal Flavin Ltd
100/101 North Main Street,
Youghal, Co Cork.
Tel: 024 92026

Michael O'Connell Gunshop
24 Liberty Square, Thurles, Co
Tipperary.
Tel: 0504 21672

Francis Nelson & Sons Ltd
42 Castle Street & Market Street,
Sligo.
Tel: 071 2651

Barton Smith Est (1788)
Hyde Bridge, Sligo.
Tel: 071 2356

SUGGESTED READING LIST

The following reading list will give further information on clay shooting:

Clay Target Shooting, Paul Bentley
A Manual of Clayshooting, Chris Cradock
Modern Clay Pigeon Shooting, Michael Raymont and Colin Jones
Shooting Made Easy, Mike Barnes
Shooting Times (weekly) covers all aspects of shooting plus results and fixtures of clay shoots.
Shooting Magazine (monthly) gives up-to-date coverage of all forms of clay shooting with a comprehensive guide to clay clubs, fixtures and results.

INDEX